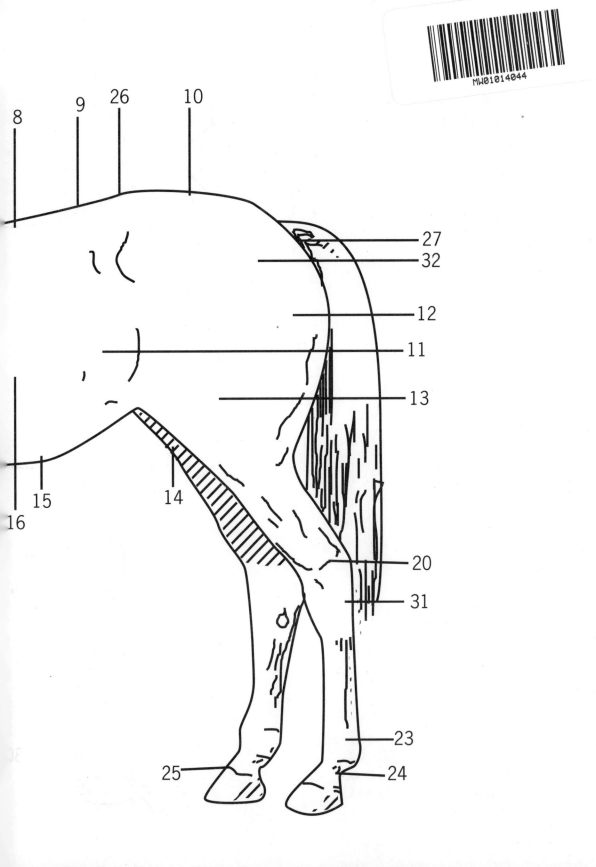

8
9
26
10
27
32
12
11
13
15
14
16
20
31
23
25
24

The Fundamentals Of
RIDING

LUCY REES

THE FUNDAMENTALS OF RIDING.
Copyright © 1991 Roxby Paintbox Company
Text copyright © 1991 Lucy Rees
The right of Lucy Rees to be identified as the author
of this work has been asserted by her in accordance
with the Copyright, Design and Patents Act, 1988.

Created and produced by Roxby Paintbox Company
Ltd, 126 Victoria Rise, London SW4 0NW.

Design Lynne Brown
Editor Elizabeth Drury
Typesetting and page make-up Eric Drewery

Printed and bound by Cayfosa, Spain

Library of Congress Cataloging-in-Publication Data
Rees. Lucy
    The fundamentals of riding / Lucy Rees
        p.   cm.
    ISBN 0-312-06750-X
    1. Horsemanship   I. Title
    SF309.R39 1991   91-24043
    798.2'3 —dc20   CIP

First U.S. Edition 1991
10 9 8 7 6 5 4 3 2 1

Acknowledgements

For their kindness, patience and generosity in discussion I would particularly like to thank: Francisco Concella d'Abreu, Anadia, Portugal; Moisie Barton, Shrewton, Wiltshire; Pam and Paul Brown, Zara Trading Centre, Sidlesham; Richard Eastwood, Cwm Pennant; Susie Elwes, Roxby Press; W.H. Giddens Saddlers Ltd, London; Ann Gittins, Dolgellau; Sylvia Loch, Sudbury; Pamela Price, Beddgelert; Carlos Eurico Marques, Estarreja, Portugal; Eleanor Russell, Cardiff; Sheelagh Stephens, Llandecwyn; Mike Tytherleigh, Wrexham.

Horse Riding
Marco Marques 1, 3, 12-13, 50, 57, 114-5, 117; Edward Boon 7; Pam Brown 14-15, 54-5, 71, 82-3, 89, 140-7; Emily Marshall 16-17, 28-9, 34-5, 38, 46-7, 58, 64-5, 94, 100-1, 130-1; Jonty Evans 18-19, 32-3, 52-3; Seamus O'Neill 20-1; Louise Gittins 22-3, 80, 84-9; Ann Gittins 24-5, 30-1, 40-1, 60-1, 74-7, 106-7, 110; Cader Vaulting Group 26-7, 40-5; Tonia Tardival 36-7; Dylan Marshall 39, 46-7, 67-8, 85, 94; Harriet Stephens 40; Caroline Pugh 51, 102-3, 138; Hannah Burgon 52; Lucy Jackson 58, 118-9, 150-1; Caroline Todd 59, 128, 136-7; William and Megan Gritten 62; Geoff Edwards 63, 98-9, 105, 112-3, 120-2; Louise Barton 86, 90-1, 128-9, 132-7; Heron Evers 92, 123; Lucy Price 105, 108, 118-9; Eurico Marques 116.

Photography
Antony Parks 8-11, 20-3, 26-7, 30-3, 46-53, 66-73, 78-9, 82-9, 92-3, 96-9, 102-7, 112-3, 120-3, 138-9, 148-9, 150-3; Charles Best 14-15, 24-5, 52-5, 58-61, 70-1, 74-7, 86-9, 90-1, 124-5, 128-9, 132-7, 140-51; Steve Peake 26-7, 38-45, 58-9, 62-9, 84-5, 94-5, 100-1, 104-5, 108-11, 118-9, 130-1, 148-9; Lucy Rees 12-13, 56-7, 115-9, 122-3.

Horses
Lipizzaner x Welsh cob 6, 16, 27-8, 34, 40, 48, 64, 72, 78, 92, 96, 100, 123, 148, 150, 154.
Welsh ponies 9, 46, 138.
Arab cross 10, 36, 38, 50, 62, 66, 68, 72, 78, 84, 102, 153.
Arab 12, 54, 70, 82, 104, 140-5.
Thoroughbred 18, 20, 32, 52, 108.
Lipizzaner 22, 30, 60, 72, 76, 80, 106, 110.
Connemara 26, 40, 42, 44.
Lusitano 56, 62, 98, 104, 112, 114, 117, 120, 122.
Hanoverian 59, 118.
TB x Connemara 59, 86, 90, 124-9, 134, 136.
Saddlebred x quarter horse 89, 146.
Welsh cob 95, 130.
Anglo Arab 116.
Hunter 133.
Akhal-Teke 152.

Contents

Partnership

You and your horse are completely different kinds of animal. You have different pleasures and fears, different views on how the world looks and what life is about. Yet a good rider and his horse act more like one animal than two. Their aims and movements seem to fuse together. How are you to learn to do this? How are you to think about riding?

Riding is a partnership. The horse lends you his strength, speed and grace, which are greater than yours. For your part you give him your guidance, intelligence and understanding, which are greater than his. Together you can achieve a richness that alone neither can.

When you work in harmony with your partner, you also increase each other's gifts. A well-ridden horse becomes more beautiful, his movements more elegant and brilliant. A true rider becomes more thoughtful, wiser and more sensitive. To reach this harmony is your aim, whatever type of riding you want to do.

At first it seems unlikely that two such different animals could work so closely together. But you are alike in some ways. You both understand the idea of living and working with other animals, for you both live in groups. You both like reward and praise; you both dislike being shouted at or punished, especially if it is for being afraid or for not understanding.

A horse does not have your powers of reasoning, and often he does not understand what it is you want to do or why. But despite his great strength and energy, he is a sensitive, peace-loving creature. It is his sensitivity that makes your partnership possible; and your sensitivity must match his. If you cannot feel what he is doing or notice his signals, he soon ignores you, just as you soon give up trying to work with someone who will not listen to you. A badly ridden horse tries to escape from his clumsy rider. If he cannot, he becomes sullen, insensitive and dull.

Two great enemies of sensitivity are tension and ignorance. When you are tense, you do not feel things delicately, nor do you control your movements well. Walking on a high bar, you keep your balance when you are calm; but when you tense up, you do not feel your loss of balance until it is almost too late. Your muscles jerk instead of reacting smoothly; you wobble and fall off. Your delicacy is lost. The same is true when you ride; and it is true of tense horses.

The more you learn about your partner, from the ground as well as on his back, the more relaxed you will be in his company. Watch him, learning to recognize his signals of pleasure, annoyance, doubt and fear; find out how and where he likes to be touched, and how to move his body about by pushing gently at him. Explore his reactions, and think about what you find. One thing you will soon learn is that horses dislike tense people: learn to be acceptable to your partner, so he works happily with you.

When you start riding, do not take on too much at once, or you will not be able to relax and feel what is happening. The more time you spend on mastering the basic ideas, the faster you will progress later.

This book is arranged to help you learn in stages. Each section covers an important idea or principle, looking first at how the horse moves by himself, then at how you affect his movement, and finally at how you put this into practice. It is best that you read through each section as a whole so that you follow the development of the ideas. The photographs have been specially taken to help you understand what you see and feel. To use them well, look particularly at the horse's balance, and at how he is using his back and back legs.

The horse's world

Horses were not put on the earth for us to enjoy. Even when we breed them for that purpose, we cannot change the fact that, like other animals, they evolved to suit a particular style of living, one in which we did not feature. Their struggle to stay alive shaped their minds and behaviour as well as their bodies. Only when you consider the world from this point of view can you understand your partner.

This group of hardy little horses lives the natural way, on a vast area of mountain. They have a huge variety of grasses, herbs, shrubs and trees to eat. The black horse is a stallion; the others are mares and youngsters. Horses always stick together in groups if they can. In the back of their minds is an age-old fear of being hunted by wolves, lions and tigers that even tame horses never really lose. They feel safer when there are others about to warn them of danger while they rest or eat.

The stallion, always the most alert, has spotted a possible tiger far away. Seeing his interest, the mares on the left turn to watch too. Horses are extraordinarily quick to spot signs of nervousness or possible danger, which always make them want to run away. This is why you should always be calm when dealing with them. Like other plant-eaters, they are not natural fighters, and they have no good way of defending themselves except by speedy escape.

Horses like resting in high places like this, where they can spot danger from far off. Being shut in, especially alone, is quite unnatural for them. Many of them are forced to get used to it, but they find it a strain. Being cave-dwellers, we tend to forget that they feel safer and more relaxed when they know they can escape.

Running away depends on having good feet, so horses are specially careful about their feet. They hate treading on anything that might hurt or trap their feet, like bogs, rocky streams, hollow-sounding bridges, wire or even fallen

jockeys. They like to follow paths they know are safe. This mountain is criss-crossed with little paths that these horses know so well that they could use them at a flat-out gallop in the dark if they had to.

The herd has a leader (here the silver-maned mare on the left), usually an older mare, bold and wise, who leads the group to new grazing, water or shelter. The younger and more timid horses trust her and readily follow her leadership. The stallion's task is to keep the herd together and stop other stallions from stealing his mares. Some horses always stay together anyway: horses make strong friendships. The two mares on the right are scratching each other's necks in a common gesture of friendship. We often notice these strong friendships in tame horses. When we keep horses together, we also often notice that one becomes a bully about food or attention. The other horses try to avoid the bullying. In

natural conditions, bullies do not often exist because there is rarely anything to fight over.

You, too, can be bully, leader or friend to your horse. If you bully him, he will want to avoid you, though he may do what you ask if he cannot escape. If you are a good leader, wise, dependable and calm, he will follow you through thick and thin without your having to bully him. Horses are natural followers. To a horse, his friend is one who is there all the time, which you are unlikely to be unless you are travelling together. But if you want to develop your friendship, note that horse-friends touch, rub and scratch each other often (and they do not feed each other tit-bits).

Like other animals that live in groups, horses have many ways of telling each other what they feel. By the way he is standing, the stallion is showing the mares that something strange has appeared. If they ignored him, he would probably move jerkily so that they noticed. Your horse will do the same to you. Unless he has learned that it is not worth while trying to communicate with you, your horse will use the same 'language' to you as he does to other horses. He uses his ears, face, tail, the way he stands or moves, and his calls, to signal playfulness, boredom, fear, annoyance, loneliness and many other feelings. Learning to recognize these signals and to understand his reasons are an important part of horsemanship.

It is also important to realize that horses' eyes do not work quite the same as ours. A horse needs to be able to move his head in order to focus on near or distant things. If he cannot raise his head on approaching a jump, or cannot put it down when picking his way over difficult ground, he cannot see properly and may refuse to go. When riding or leading a horse, always give his head freedom, or he is half-blind.

THE FIRST PRINCIPLE
Free forward movement

The first principle of riding is that of free forward movement. It is only when the horse moves forward freely that his side of the partnership, his gifts of strength, energy and grace, can be fully realized and turned to your advantage.

The horse on the right is galloping freely. Although he can move freely at slow paces too, you can see the changes in his body most clearly at this fast pace. One complete stride is shown.

At first he pulls himself into a tight ball, with his nose tucked in. In the middle of the stride he is fully stretched out; then he gathers himself together again ready for the next stride.

At the gallop he puts his feet down one at a time, starting with the back one. It is his back feet that thrust him forward. When he is moving freely, at any pace, he reaches his back feet well forward under his body. As he does this, his back rises. He coils it under him, dropping his bottom. You can see his hip rise as he puts weight on his back leg. For a brief moment his weight is on his back legs; then he rolls forward on to his outstretched front ones. You can see how his balance tips from back to front, then back again. You can see, too, how he brings his nose in when he shortens his back, and stretches forward as he reaches forward with his front legs.

If you are to ride this horse, you must not interfere with the fluid rhythm of his movements or his freedom will be lost. Your weight must be so perfectly balanced that you do not unbalance him, even when he rocks forward and back. You must move with him, flowing with his movements: the rise and fall of his back, the thrust of his hindquarters, the movement of his head and neck.

The horse is an athlete. He cannot perform well with a stiff weight unbalancing him. When you give a small child a piggyback, the same is true for you. It is only when he is balanced and moves with you that you can move properly.

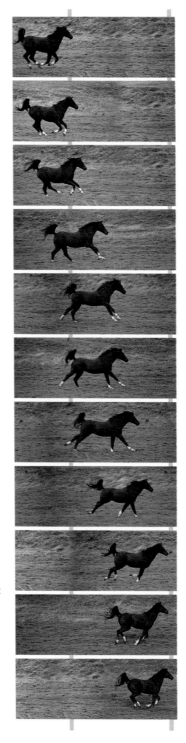

As the horse flies through the air he is raising his back and tucking his bottom under him, reaching forward with his back feet.

His left back foot touches down first, right under the middle of his body. He brings the other legs forward as he balances on it.

His right back and left front feet are moving forward together; his right back foot is about to touch down, almost under his shoulder.

As he rolls forward on to his right back foot he begins to lengthen his body, reaching his left front foot forward.

Now his right back foot is carrying his whole weight, pushing him forward.

He is now at full stretch; his back has dropped; his neck and head reach forward as his left front foot touches down.

On a diagonal pair of legs, he rolls his weight forward towards his outstretched right front leg.

He rocks on to his front legs as his back legs lift off behind.

Still leaning forward, he carries all his weight on his right front leg and starts to bring his back legs forward.

He begins to change his balance, shortening his neck as he brings his back legs under him.

As his right front leg lifts off he is again flying. His left back foot will strike down well in front of his right front hoofprint.

How are you to sit on this horse?

Balance, suppleness and rhythm are the keys to sitting well. Sitting well is in itself the key to good riding. Most people think riding is about control. But if you sit badly the horse is uncontrolled himself. As he staggers to keep his balance, his movements are clumsy and graceless. Your task in controlling them is made a thousand times more difficult. When you sit well on a happy, free-moving horse, the problem of control almost vanishes. You seem to fuse together.

The best way to learn to sit well is on a horse that someone else is controlling. Free of worries about what the horse is going to do, you can also be free from tension as you allow your body to develop balance, suppleness and rhythm. You also learn to feel exactly what the horse is doing, which is an important part of riding.

However, there are different ways of sitting ('seats') for different styles of riding. In all of them the rider is as balanced as on his own two feet on the floor; his point of balance is above the horse's; and he moves with the horse's movement. But the exact way in which he does this depends on the work he wants the horse to do: slow, delicate work on flat ground or galloping round a cross-country course, herding cattle or winning races. There is no one 'correct' seat; each different way of sitting works differently, and what is correct in one is not necessarily correct in another. This is sometimes confusing for the beginner. The next ten pages show how the different seats work at the canter or gallop.

The classical seat

The classical seat was first described by the Greek general and horsemaster Xenophon in 400 BC: 'as though a man were standing upright with his legs apart'. As Greek friezes show, most Greeks rode with a 'chair' seat, with their bottoms further back and their knees hitched up. Although it the most natural way for an untutored man to ride a bareback horse, Xenophon saw that it unbalanced both horse and rider, making delicate control impossible. The classical seat allowed much finer and more athletic riding.

The art of classical riding, which is like a slow, beautifully rhythmic ballet, was redeveloped in the seventeenth and eighteenth centuries in Europe. Many of the exercises are refined versions of the movements a knight would find handy in battle. Today it exists in its purest form in Spain, Portugal (where the movements are used in bullfighting), Austria and Hungary, where the old classical breeds, Andalusian, Lusitano and Lipizzan, are used. Modern 'dressage' (from the French *dresser*, to train) differs slightly in emphasis and style

The classical or dressage saddle is scooped out so that you sit deep into it, with your point of balance above the horse's. The stirrups hang under the balls of your feet when your legs are hanging vertically. (Many people find it difficult to spread their legs so wide at first, and tend to stick their knees forward to relieve the strain, so this is a good check that your feet are in the right place.) The rider above is using a classical Portuguese saddle.

since the horses used are larger and of different natural talent.

The horse above is cantering slowly. The rider sits tall and proud, as if honoured to be riding him. Yet there is no stiffness or tension anywhere in his body. By keeping his legs vertical he has to spread them wide round the horse's barrel, so he is sitting on a broad area of buttock and crotch. As long as he keeps his balance and moves with the horse, gravity keeps him on it.

His legs fold softly round the horse so that the heel hangs clear unless he wants to press it in to the horse's side. He does not grip it at all. 'One of the key points', says Nuno d'Oliveira, the greatest modern classical master, 'is the entire relaxation of the rider's leg'.

Relaxation from the waist down means that his hips and legs move with the horse. Carrying himself proudly from the waist up means that his upper half remains still. Between these two parts, at the waist and in the small of his back, he is loose and supple. This free-moving link swings with each swing of the horse's stride,

absorbing the movement of the horse's back. If he were stiff, as most beginners are, he would not be able to keep his bottom in the saddle, or would rock his shoulders to and fro. If he leaned forward, or slumped, he would also lose the free movement of his spine.

His confidence in his balance means that his shoulders, arms and hands are also relaxed and supple, so that his touch on the reins is tender and delicate.

His stirrups are so long that they serve only to stop the front of his foot from flopping down. They give him no support whatsoever.

The advantage of the classical seat is its reliance on balance and suppleness rather than grip. Free of any tension, the rider can feel every movement of the horse's spine and hips through his bottom and spine. The long relaxed leg also gives the rider the maximum feel and control.

The disadvantage is that the rider's bottom must always stay in the saddle. This is not really possible on a horse moving fast and freely over rough ground, and in jumping it actually hinders the horse.

The Western seat

When the Spaniards colonized Mexico and what are now the south-western States, from the sixteenth century onwards, they took with them their superb horses, their classical style of riding and their deep-seated, high-backed saddles. As cattle-herding developed, the classical style and saddle were changed to suit the working cowboy. (The horse, too, changed, becoming stockier.) Nevertheless, many of the characteristics of the classical seat remain: the proud, upright way of sitting; the loose, supple waist; the long leg; the reliance on balance rather than grip.

The horse on the opposite page is in an easy canter or lope (from the Spanish *galop*).

Like the classical rider, the Western rider absorbs the movement of the horse's back in the small of his back. For this he needs to carry himself tall, so that his back is stretched and free. His stirrups are so long that by straightening his legs he would barely rise from the saddle. He might do this at a flat-out gallop; otherwise he sits at all times.

The heel should be under the rider's hip. In practice many working cowboys tend to push the lower leg forward and brace themselves against the back of the saddle when roping cattle. This can mean that the seat is unbalanced backward, throwing too much weight on to the rear of the horse. The shape of the quarter-horse, which is low-withered, and the fast work it needs to do, mean that this unbalancing is no great fault, as it might be in other forms of riding. The sturdy saddle prevents any damage to the horse's back.

The Western rider is firm in the saddle but does not grip with his legs. They are relaxed, hanging naturally with the toe pointing forward and the heel slightly down. The rider's firmness is given by the large area of contact with his horse. Western horses are broad and solid, which helps. So does the saddle.

The Western rider shown here rides with both reins loosely held in the left hand. Because of the saddlehorn, she carries her hand higher than in other styles. This again is not the fault it would be in other forms of riding, where a snaffle bit is used; for the Western rider uses a curb or a hackamore, which tends to lower the horse's head (see page 150). He barely uses the bit anyway; instead, he uses a neck rein, his weight and often his voice so that, although the bit is of a harsher type, the horse very seldom, if ever, feels it.

Today there are few genuine cowponies: many different specialities, often with their own

A Western saddle is solid enough to hold a struggling steer anchored to the horn. The rear cinch (girth) only tightens when the saddle threatens to tip forward (see page 141). This is a roping saddle: the swells beneath the horn are undercut so the rope does not snag.

forms of competition, have emerged. But the traditional Western view of the horse as a true working partner remains the strongest influence in training. Western riding, with its emphasis on solving practical problems swiftly and calmly, is the easiest and most comfortable of all styles for horse and rider. Its main disadvantage is that you (the rider, not the horse) may find it difficult to adapt to other styles. The massive saddle gives you so much security that you may not develop a truly balanced seat, and you may find lighter saddles difficult to stay on.

Western riding is examined in more detail on pages 140 – 147.

The central seat

This way of sitting is sometimes called, rather vaguely and confusingly, 'balanced', 'all-purpose' or simply 'correct'. Here it is called 'central' because it is the least specialized of all seats, the most central of a wide variety.

In the eighteenth century, the development of artillery guns that would pierce even the heaviest armour made the cavalry change their tactics. They abandoned lances, armour and great clumsy horses in favour of swifter action on lighter, nimbler steeds. The armoured knights used to lean backward to withstand the brutal impact of the lance; the new cavalry could use a better-balanced seat that gave more precise control and tired the horse less. But they found that true classical riding, which uses only slow paces and flat ground, was unsuited to charging over hillsides, so they worked out a more general-purpose way of sitting.

This horse is cantering freely. One complete stride is shown.

The rider here sits with her knee more bent (*a la jinnetta*) than in the classical seat, but with shoulder, hip and heel in one straight line so that she is well balanced. She carries herself proudly, neither stiffly nor slumped. Her waist and the small of her back are stretched and free. It is this part that moves with the movement of the horse's back. Her shoulders are still; her upper arms hang loosely. Her wrists and hands are relaxed and loose, so that when the horse moves freely her hands move gently with the movement of his head.

She sits right down on her bottom, crotch and thighs, as in the classical seat. She does not try to grip with her knees, which would push her upwards out of the saddle. But her knees are firm on the saddle because her weight is on her heel, not on the stirrup. Dropping her heel changes the shape of the muscles in the thigh, pulling the knee in. The more she puts her weight on her heel, the firmer her knee.

Her stirrups are just short enough for her to stand clear of the saddle. If she does this, her heel will drop even more, pulling her knee in still further.

Her toes point forward. She does not grip with her calf: this would be a serious mistake as

'General-purpose' saddles vary a good deal: in some the flaps go further forward and are padded. They are more suitable for fast cross-country work. This type, rather flat in the seat, offers you little help but stops you sitting too far back. It is an ideal beginner's saddle, for it will make you develop a good seat rather than relying on the saddle to keep you on the horse.

it would ask the horse to go faster and faster. She can swing the lower part of her leg freely without affecting her seat, her security, or the firmness of her knee.

This rider looks completely free and confident. You can see that taking her reins away would make no difference to her. This is what is meant by an 'independent' seat: her security does not depend on her hands. Achieving an independent seat, so that you do not keep your balance by hanging on to your reins, is any rider's first aim.

The great advantage of learning the central seat first is that you can ride any horse, anywhere in the world, however specialized its training, with a fair degree of success. This is not true of the more specialized seats. You can also learn the other seats easily.

In the later part of this section we examine the central seat in much greater detail, showing you how it works at the different paces and how to go about practising while someone else controls the horse. This is the seat you are recommended to use in everyday riding.

The forward seat

The forward seat is a special-purpose jumping seat developed by Caprilli, an Italian Army captain, in the 1900s. At the time the cavalry were increasingly interested in jumping fences. The only riders who regularly jumped large jumps were English and Irish huntsmen, who rode with a clearly unbalanced 'chair' seat, leaning back as they took off. This caused the horses great strain in the back, loins and hind legs and, as the riders often kept their balance by leaning back on the reins, the horses' mouths were damaged and hardened: hence the English development of powerful hunters, the ironmongery to stop them, and great veterinary skill.

Cavalrymen using the English method found it hard to get their horses to jump more than a metre in cold blood. Caprilli watched horses jumping far higher when they were not being ridden and realized how much the riders were hindering their horses. He saw that to clear a large jump the horse must be free in his back and loins, to get his back legs under him. He must be free to change his balance suddenly and dramatically, and he must also be allowed to stretch his head and neck as he reaches out with his front legs. Caprilli saw that this freedom could only be given when the rider took his weight off the horse's back by rising from the saddle.

The horse above is cantering freely. The photographs show him through one stride.

At the canter or gallop the rider's weight is not on the saddle but on his knees and heels. He absorbs the rise and fall of the horse's back by bobbing on his thighs, not in the small of his back, so that his head remains at the same height. His bottom does not touch the saddle, or he would bang the horse's back. Especially in the moment when he coils his back.

He does not try to spread his legs wide, like the classical rider, but keeps them in; and his weight is on his heels, not the stirrups. Both these actions increase the firm hold of his knees which, being normally slightly above the widest point of the horse's barrel, tighten still more. Thus his 'grip' is not so much a conscious action as the mechanical effect of having his stirrups short.

Although he leans his upper body forward, he is balanced over his heels. A vertical line through his body shows that he has pushed his hips back so that there is as much weight behind his heels as in front. But he can easily shift his weight forward or back to follow the flow of the horse's movement and the swift changes of balance and angle seen especially in jumping. The horse is thus much freer to use his body as he wants.

As you can see, the difference between this and the central seat is more than a matter of simply shortening the stirrups. You have to learn to position your legs differently and use your balance differently. Unfortunately, some riders try to combine the two styles and end up

The jumping saddle has forward-cut flaps that allow for the rider's knee position. They are heavily padded in front, for when you land after jumping high and fast the impact on your knees is tremendous. The stirrups are of a special kind: the eye through which the stirrup leather goes is not in the middle but off-set, so that the tread of the stirrup hangs at an angle, not flat. The outside edge of the foot is then higher than the inside, which helps to push the knee in.

sitting on the back of the saddle because their stirrups are too short. This is the unbalanced chair seat that does nobody, least of all the horse, any good.

The forward seat is specially designed for jumping or fast cross-country work. Its disadvantage is that because the rider's back is not free, as in the central seat, it is tiring when used for long periods. Moreover, the rider is not in contact with the horse's back, so he loses some of the feeling of what the horse is doing, and some of the means of controlling it.

The forward seat is examined in more detail on pages 128 – 129.

19

The racing seat

Until the end of the nineteenth century jockeys rode with long stirrups. But at the turn of the century the American Tod Sloan, inspired, so he said, by the Sioux Amerindian style of riding, revolutionized the racing seat. He shortened his stirrups until he was perched 'like a monkey up a stick', crouching along the horse's neck. The advantage of this style, which like the forward seat frees the horse's back, was immediately obvious: the horse could gallop faster and further. Within a few years every jockey did the same. Modern flat-race jockeys ride even shorter, though when jumping or exercising most jockeys ride at a safer length.

The jockey rides knock-kneed, as shown on the right: the more he keeps his heels out, the more secure he is. The shorter his stirrups, the more the barrel of the horse splays his feet apart, increasing the knock-kneed effect. By crouching forward he puts his main weight on his knees, until he is almost kneeling on the horse's shoulders.

The jockey copes with the horse's movement like the forward seat rider, by bobbing on his thighs. The movement of the horse's shoulder against his knee and lower leg makes the rhythm easily felt. This jockey has gauged the horse's movement so beautifully that his head is moving in a perfect horizontal line. He rises as the horse

The saddle is small, and designed to be light rather than to help the jockey: it is hardly more than just an anchor for the stirrups. The splendid shoulder and barrel of the Thoroughbred provide a natural dip into which the knee fits against the forward-cut flap. But there are no knee-rolls for security. The jump jockey must therefore push his feet forward and lean back when landing from a jump, unlike the showjumper, for otherwise the impact of landing would throw him forward. The pad underneath carries handicap weights.

drops his back and extends, and crouches as the horse rises. Thus he appears to keep still.

The Thoroughbred's long neck extends and retracts a great deal during each stride, and the jockey needs to move his hands forward and back as much as half a metre to keep the same pressure on the rein. The horse needs this pressure: a racehorse 'takes a hold' on the bit, leaning on it to help his balance. If the jockey were to let go suddenly, the horse would tip forward. If he did not keep the pressure precise and steady, the horse could not keep a good galloping rhythm. Despite the fact that he rides with a constant pressure, the jockey's hands need to be just as sensitive as any other rider's.

The jockey is admirably positioned to shift his weight, which is slight compared to that of the horse, so as to have the greatest effect on the horse's back and on his speed. As the jockey never puts his bottom in the saddle, and cannot use his legs, these shifts of weight forwards and backwards are one of the main ways he can influence the horse.

The advantage of this seat is that it gives the horse freedom to use his body to the full. Notice that this horse, the same one as on the previous page, sprang into a gallop without being urged. When he was ridden in other styles, he was quite content merely to canter.

The central seat: how to sit

It was said of d'Oliveira that he rode his horses as if he were a king, and so they carried him as if he were a king. Any horse will be able to carry you well and will move beautifully if you sit proudly, and are well balanced and supple. The greatest difficulty is to be free from tension anywhere in your body.

Look at this rider. She sits straight, yet she is not stiff. Her legs seem to fold round the horse without clinging. She looks soft and supple without seeming sloppy. Both she and the horse look calm and ready.

When you get on a horse, remember this look of calmness and pleasure. Breathe slowly and deeply, concentrating on feeling that the centre of your being is in a point just below your navel. This is a technique used in yoga and many Eastern martial arts. In riding, your centre will be free. Above it, you grow upwards, like a plant; below it, you flow downwards.

With your feet out of the stirrups, wriggle from side to side in the saddle, with your legs completely relaxed. You will then find the deepest part of the saddle, where your balance is above the horse's. You will probably be able to put your hand flat between the back of your bottom and the back of the saddle. Now stretch your legs straight out sideways, as if you were doing the splits, then let them rest gently against the horse's sides. You should be able to feel that your weight is pressing your pelvis, or hip girdle, against the saddle in three places: in the middle at the front, and on your two seat bones further back. If you rock to and fro, you will feel more weight go on to the front, then on to the back. Settle so that your weight is even on all three points. Take your time to feel what is happening, for the way you get your hips settled affects everything else.

Without tightening yourself, grow upwards

from this firm base. Do not raise yourself from the saddle: from below the waist you belong to the horse, but above it you carry yourself. Your spine is a column of little bones separated by softer cushions (discs) that absorb any jarring. This column naturally curves slightly inwards at the small of your back when you stand 'straight'. But if you are slumped, or leaning forward, the springy curve is not there, and the cushions are not in the right place to work properly. If you are then jogged, it is desperately uncomfortable, like jumping from a height with your legs straight. You tense up against the shock, which makes matters worse. So it is important to stretch your back so that the links of the curve, and the cushions between them, can work properly.

For the moment, ignore your hands. Put them on top of your head or behind your back, or let them hang. Do not clutch on to anything with them. It is important that you first learn to ride without them, so that you develop your balance and seat.

Imagine your legs are boneless sacks of sand. They do not cling to the horse: they reach for the ground. Since the horse is in the way, your weight keeps you on. If your legs are hanging straight, the stirrups will be just above the balls of your feet. If your feet are further forward than that, open your legs wide, draw them back and try again. Slip your feet in, rest the balls of your feet on the stirrups and drop your weight into your heels. This is important since it keeps your knees close to the saddle without gripping. If you grip, you push your bottom up out of the saddle, as you will see by trying. If you stand on your toes rather than your heels, your knees come off the saddle. As long as your feet are underneath you, you will not lose the stirrups. Try to ride with them as

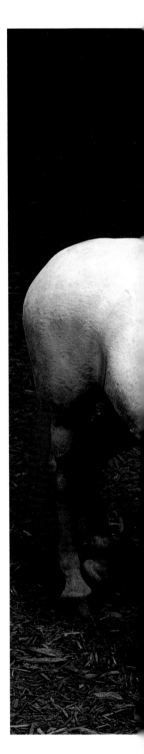

Your weight rests above the strongest part of the horse's back.

long as is comfortable: the bottom of the stirrup should be about level with your ankle bone when your leg is hanging long and relaxed. If your stirrups are too short (a common beginner's mistake), you will push your bottom backward in the saddle and will have to lean forward to keep your balance, so your suppleness will be lost.

Your toes should point forward, not out. If they point out, you will clutch with your lower leg, which is a dreadful mistake as the horse will go faster and faster. Your lower leg should be able to swing freely without your knee coming away from the saddle.

You may find that the inside of your thigh seems to push your knee away from the saddle so that it sticks out, while your heel goes in. You need to turn your hip joint inwards. Take hold of the inside of your thigh from behind, and pull it down and out until your thigh bone rests against the saddle. Another way is to stand in the stirrups, turn your toes and knees right in, and sit down again. This may feel uncomfortable for you at first but, as your tendons and ligaments stretch, it will feel more natural.

Apart from being generally too tense, most beginners tend to lean forward without realizing it. This is partly a natural reaction to fear, and partly because your body is not very good at telling where it is unless your feet are on the ground. Have someone check your position. Another common mistake is to have the leg too far forward. If you can see your toes, your feet are too far forward; but have it checked that your shoulder, hip and heel are in a straight line. This puts the curve of your back right for absorbing movement.

Above all, feel proud and happy: hold your head high and your body will naturally hold itself well.

Mounting and dismounting

When you are about to ride a horse, even if it is a riding-school horse that has been handed to you saddled and bridled, remember that this is a partnership, however brief. The horse will want to know who you are. So stand by him, quite relaxed, and let him hear your voice; scratch his neck and shoulder. This is a natural sign of friendship to him. Let him smell you. Let yourself get to know him calmly.

Check that the girth is done up properly. Many horses take a deep breath when first girthed up, so the saddle is loose when they breathe out. Check that the stirrups are about the right length by putting your fingertips on the bar that holds the stirrup leather and holding

Do not bang his back as you sit down.

Raise your right leg over the horse's back, high enough so you do not kick him, turn and sit softly.

Catch the far side of the seat of the saddle in your right hand as you go up.

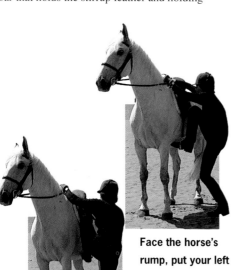

Face the horse's rump, put your left foot in the stirrup, bounce on your right foot and spring upwards.

Take both reins in your left hand, with a piece of mane or the front of the saddle to steady your hand.

the stirrup against your arm. If the bottom of the stirrup fits into your armpit when your arm and fingers are straight, it will be about right.

We usually mount from the left side, a habit arising from the time when gentlemen wore swords on their left hips and found they got in the way when they mounted from the right. It is as well to practise mounting from either side.

Do not try to get on facing the horse's side or you will stick your toe in and he will walk off with you hopping alongside.

Note that although this is a strong horse, and the rider light, the horse has swung his head and neck to the left as his balance is thrown to that side. If you *haul* yourself up, rather than spring, you unbalance the horse so badly that he

Take both feet out of the stirrups.

Swing your legs forward and then quickly back as you lean forward.

and use it to help you, but take care you do not pull at the reins.

Western-style. Most Westerners face forward, jump into the stirrups and use the horn to pull themselves up in one smooth movement, but you will find the European way easier at first. In dismounting, it is difficult to kick your leg over the high back of the saddle, so hold the horn, leave your left foot in the stirrup and step down on to your right foot. This method is not used on other saddles because you are momentarily in a dangerous position when you are half way off: if the horse moved suddenly, you would fall on your back.

will stagger or may strain his back. If you have little spring, practise bouncing up on to a chair at home.

Other ways of getting on and off

Having a leg-up. Face the horse's side and bend your left leg back at the knee. Your helper should put one hand under your knee and the other under your shin. Count to three and spring up off your right leg. If you kick with your left leg too, you will boot your helper as he boosts you up.

Jumping on bareback. Face the horse's side, take a chunk of mane and your reins in your left hand, and put your right hand flat on his loins. Jump so that you are lying on your belly over the horse, then put your right leg over his back. If he is small enough, you will find that you can get your left elbow the other side of his neck

Your right leg should kick high over his rump to join your left.

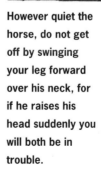

However quiet the horse, do not get off by swinging your leg forward over his neck, for if he raises his head suddenly you will both be in trouble.

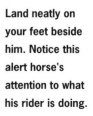

Land neatly on your feet beside him. Notice this alert horse's attention to what his rider is doing.

Supple and free: exercises

These simple exercises stretch your legs, so that you can find it easier to spread them wide. Left to right: kneeling with one leg stretched behind; splits; tailor seat (this is particularly good for stiff hips); touching ground.

To sit down well on a horse you need to be free in your hip, so that you can spread your legs wide and have a broad base to sit on. To cope with the horse's movement you need to be supple in your waist. To balance well you need to carry yourself well. To keep your weight in your heel, using your ankle as a shock-absorber, you need supple ankles. To hold the reins sensitively you need relaxed arms and wrists. If you are stiff on the ground, you will be worse on a horse.

It is a good idea, then, to loosen your hips, back and ankles when you are nowhere near a horse, and pay attention to the way you hold yourself. When you are on a horse, there are many exercises that help you lose your natural tension, too. Adults are usually much stiffer than children, so never consider yourself too old for such games.

Stretching the ligaments in your legs by doing the exercises shown will help supple you. High kicks also loosen your hips.

Here are some other ground exercises that will help your riding improve between lessons.
1. Stand with your back to a wall, so that the backs of your heels, your bottom and your shoulders touch the wall. Your knees should be slightly bent. This is your riding position. Put yourself in it many times a day, and your body will learn the feel of the position. If you put a book under your toes, you will be standing on your heels too, learning how to drop your weight into your heels.
2. Think about the way you walk. If you are round-shouldered, or if you slump or lean forward from the hip, you will not miraculously improve by getting on a horse. Carry yourself straight but not tensely, shoulders straight but relaxed and low, and let your hips move as loosely as you can. Walking with a book on your head helps.
3. Stand with the balls of your feet on a stair, let your ankles relax, and drop your weight into your heels. If you put your weight first on to

your toe, then on to your heel, you can feel the change in your balance, and in the shape of your thigh and calf.

4. Dance in front of a mirror with your feet apart, keeping your shoulders and feet still but letting your middle wiggle about as much as possible. Throw away your inhibitions and self-consciousness, and have a good time with a strong rock beat.

Once you are on a horse, try the exercises shown. You can do them bareback or with a saddle; but do make sure someone is holding the horse lest you surprise him.

1. Hold the back of the saddle and kick your feet high over the horse's neck, clapping them together. You will have to keep your legs straight. This helps bring your bottom forward in the saddle. If the horse is not used to it, warn him first by doing it slowly and praising his patience.

2. Hold your arms out sideways and swing them forward or back. If you are not loose in the waist, your feet will move too, so practise until they keep still.

3. Swing your arm round in circles to loosen your shoulders – and watch those feet.

4. Shake your hands to loosen your wrists and fingers.

5. Lean right back until you are lying along the horse's back, with your head resting on his rump. Your feet should not come forward if your back is loose.

6. Ride with your hands on top of your head or behind your head, or touching your shoulders. Keep your arms back so you cannot see your elbows, then your shoulders are in the right place.

7. Ride with your arms straight out ahead, like the girl in the picture. If your shoulders are still but you are moving in the waist, your hands

Putting your feet up behind the saddle pulls your knees back into the right position. When you drop your feet, do not let your knees come forward. Note the good curve in the rider's back.

When touching your toe, make sure your opposite leg does not go back into the pony's side. When you can do this, touch your opposite toe.

will stay still. This is an excellent way to check what you are doing at the trot or canter. Even better is holding a full glass of water out at arm's length in front of you, and trying not to spill a drop.

Practise these first at a standstill and walk. As you improve, do them at faster paces, without stirrups or without a saddle. As you can see, riding while someone else is controlling the horse can be exciting and fun. The longer you stick at it, improving the way you sit and move, the easier you will find it to control the horse when the time comes. Remember that it is not just doing the exercises, but *how* you do them, that counts. The idea is to be soft and relaxed, not stiff and jerky.

Your riding will also be helped by your relaxing, watching and thinking when you are around horses. Work out how they like to be touched, led and groomed, and how they use their eyes. Watch the way that good horsepeople move. They are always quiet, calm and unhurried, and horses feel safe around them.

The walk

Walking is a four-beat pace: you can hear the horse's feet go 'one-two', 'three-four'.

Here, on the right, the horse is putting down his feet in the order: right back, right front, left back, left front. As you can see, he always has two or three feet on the ground at any one time. A horse feels safest at a walk (he cannot see well if he moves fast) and will usually want to walk if he is uncertain of the ground or is in a new place.

The horse is walking freely and briskly. His back foot steps almost into the track left by the front one. This is called 'tracking up'. When he slopes along, not moving freely, he does not track up. Check your horse's hoofprints when you ride on sand or mud and you will see this.

Each time the horse thrusts himself forward with a back foot, he thrusts the rider forward too. You feel this as a series of shoves from behind. You can see this rider's supple back move in and out as she absorbs the movement.

Each time he steps forward with a front foot, the horse's head and neck stretch forward. Unless your hands move forward and back too, the rein will come tight at every step, hindering his free movement.

You can see this rider's hands move to allow for this. Her arms are loose; she holds the rein so lightly that she feels every slight movement of the horse's head through the rein. Before you try to do anything with your reins, you should make sure that your hands are light and free to give to the horse's head movements.

When you first try walking, remember that you should be sitting down on the horse, not looking for support from the stirrups. Try riding without them. Experiment with the effect of tightening your lower back and then

You will find that the horse rolls you from side to side as he walks, as shown in the pictures on the right. As he brings his back foot forward, you can feel the hip on that side rise. It falls as his foot moves back, while the other rises.

Here, the superimposed outlines of the horse's hips show how they rise and fall. You will only feel this well when your spine is upright and supple. Practise feeling this movement so that you can always tell which leg the horse is stepping on. You can feel it better going downhill, or bareback.

28

letting it swing freely. You will find that when your back is tight, the horse will tighten his back too, so that he takes smaller, slower steps. The more you let your back swing, the more his can swing, so that he strides out freely.

With experience, you will feel that the horse has different kinds of walk. He can plod along. This is not what is wanted in any kind of riding. He can walk freely and positively, as he is here. But when he sees something interesting, or when he wants to break into a trot, his head and neck come up and his whole front end seems to lift. You can feel his back rise underneath you. He suddenly feels much more powerful and energetic. This is called a 'collected' walk, because it feels as if he has pulled himself together. His steps are shorter and bouncier. You can learn how to ask a horse to walk like this.

He can also take much longer strides.

Again you can feel his back lift and work underneath you, but he wants to stretch his head forward and down more. He is most likely to do this when he wants to go home but has not been asked to trot. His steps do not go any faster but he covers more ground. This is called an 'extended' walk.

Feel the differences between these kinds of walk, and watch what happens to his hoof-prints. In an ordinary walk he just about tracks up; in a collected walk he tracks up perfectly; in an extended walk he overtracks: that is, his back foot steps further forward than his front hoofprint. (You can tell which hoofprint is which because a front shoe is round while a back one is in the shape of an egg.) The more you work at understanding and feeling what the horse is doing with his body, and the different ways he can use it, the easier you will find more advanced riding.

29

The trot: sitting

The trot is a two-time pace: you hear two beats, not four. The horse moves his left front and right back feet together (left diagonal), then his right front and left back (right diagonal). Between each step there is a moment when he bounces off the ground, with all four feet in the air. When you first trot, you can feel these regular, jarring bounces at each step. There are two ways of dealing with this: sitting or posting.

The pictures are of a sitting trot. The rider absorbs all the horse's movement in the small of her back, allowing her stomach to push forward so that the curve of her back springs in and out with each bounce. Her legs are loose, her shoulders back.

When you first try this, you are likely to be too tense. If your back is tense, it cannot act like a spring and absorb the shock. If your legs are tense, you will push your bottom out of the saddle and bounce more. If you lean forward, you will lose the arch in your back and bounce more. So keep your shoulders back and relax your legs. You may do better without stirrups, so that you are not tempted to stand on them. If you still bounce, hold the front of the saddle with one hand and pull yourself deeper into it, letting your legs hang freely and your shoulders tilt back. Lean back, but keep pushing your navel towards the horse's ears. Once you have realized you are not going to bounce off, you will relax the arch in your back and will be able to feel it working to absorb the bounce. As you get better, check that you are returning to an upright position and that your legs have not come forward. As soon as you have removed all the tension in your legs, they will hang straight.

This sitting trot is used when the horse is trotting slowly. It is always used in classical or Western riding, or when 'schooling' a horse (working him in circles or patterns designed to help his balance and suppleness). Doing a sitting trot without stirrups, letting your feet flop down, helps your position, for you cannot do it well unless you are sitting properly on your bottom and not clutching with your legs. Holding your arms out in front, and seeing if your hands go up and down, helps you check that you really are taking all the bounce in your back. Notice that in a trot the horse naturally carries his head higher and stiller than in a walk.

As with the walk, so a horse has several different types of trot. A relaxed horse will do a slow, smooth jog trot. This is what is wanted in a Western horse. But an excited or highly strung horse jogs with a high head and tense back, which should be discouraged as it is exhausting for both horse and rider. A brisker trot is the ordinary or working trot: here the hindquarters are working harder and you can feel the horse's back working too. The collected trot (which is what this horse is doing) is slower, though his hindquarters are still working hard so that his back lifts underneath you. As he shortens his back, the horse arches his neck and pulls his nose in. You may feel your horse do this when he is paying particular attention to something he is slightly scared of as he trots by. In an extended trot he lengthens his stride enormously, though his steps are not quicker. His back rises under you, but he stretches his head forward and down. Some horses and ponies do this naturally in trotting races, when they know not to break into a gallop.

Horses can also do very high, bouncy, powerful trots (*passage* and *piaffe*), but it is usually only stallions that do them naturally.

Below, two images at different stages in the stride have been superimposed. You can see how the arch in the rider's back acts as a shock-absorber as the horse bounces up and down.

In a trot most of the horse's movement is forward, and up and down. The sideways movement of the hips is not felt as well as in the walk. But in a broad-hipped horse trotting slowly you can feel which back foot, and therefore which diagonal, is going down. In narrower horses you will have to be very relaxed, and maybe lean back a little, to feel it. It helps if you keep your eyes shut. (You can also tell by watching his shoulder, but that tends to make you lean forward.)

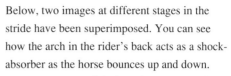

The post or rising trot

When post-boys used to deliver the mail, they trotted as fast as possible rather than galloped, for a horse galloping on uneven, rutted roads is more likely to fall. At the high speed a good trotter can go, the bounce is too much to sit to. Instead, the post-boys used the bounce to help them rise to every alternate step. This is the post or rising (also called English) trot.

Here the rider is rising from the saddle as one diagonal (the right one) hits the ground, then sitting when the the other comes down. When you get the rhythm right, the trot feels smooth. You can see that as you rise your weight drops into your heels. This is important, for it pulls your knees into the saddle and steadies you. If you rise by standing on your toes, you will lose your security and your balance.

Unless your horse has a particularly smooth, slow trot, you will probably find a rising trot easier to master than the sitting trot at first. Being relaxed and supple is not as important in this trot. First make sure that you can rise and sit down rapidly and easily at a standstill. You should not lose your balance, move your legs, make use of your hands, or thump the horse's back as you come down. You will find it easier if you concentrate on throwing your hips towards the horse's ears. Be sure that your weight is dropping into your heels so that your knees stay firm.

Now try this at a walk, counting 'one, two' as the horse's front feet come down: rise on 'one' and sit on 'two'. Then try it at a trot. If you find it difficult to rise without leaning a long way forward, your feet are probably too far forward. If you find it difficult to catch the rhythm, try holding on to a piece of mane, rising all the time until you feel the rhythm of the bounces, and sitting on every other stride. But do make sure that you can rise properly without holding

0   2.5
                   metres

anything before you ride with reins. If you use the reins to keep yourself steady, you will ruin the sensitivity of the horse's mouth. There is no need to rise very high: the higher you rise, the harder you will come down. As you get better, try to reduce the rise until you are only just clearing the saddle.

When trotting in circles, rise on the inside diagonal. In other words, if you are circling to the left, you should be rising as the left front and right back feet are going down. This helps the horse, for his right back foot must make more effort than his left: and if you take your weight off his back for that moment, you make it easier.

When you trot in a figure of eight, change the diagonal you are trotting on as you swing across the centre and change direction. All you do is sit for an extra stride, so you bounce once and then start rising again.

When you are out hacking, or trotting in straight lines, make sure that you change your diagonal from time to time so that you use both diagonals equally. This is more important than it might seem. Most people find it easier to rise on one diagonal than the other at first, and many get into the habit of using only that one. However, this means that the horse gradually develops his muscles differently on each side, with the result that he becomes lop-sided. Eventually you find that he will turn easily one way but not the other, and it becomes increasingly difficult to keep him trotting when you are using the other diagonal.

The outline of horse and rider as she rises is superimposed to show the movement of the horse's hips.

The canter

The rider above sits without bouncing by letting her back roll with the horse's. Her shoulders are still but her hands follow the movement of the horse's head. Her legs are completely relaxed. Here she is bareback and you can see that she needs neither stirrups nor saddle: her position is as on page 16, except that the front of her foot flops without the stirrup. As in the sitting trot, it is easier to sit without bouncing if the horse is moving slowly, and your back and legs are loose.

The canter is a three-beat pace, with a moment when all four feet are in the air. At other times the horse has one, two or three feet on the ground. Cantering puts more strain on a horse's legs than trotting, when the weight is always carried by two feet, never one.

This horse is said to be leading on his right foot, for you see the right one stretch forward the most. In fact, each stride begins with the opposite back leg, as in the gallop. First he coils his back under him, bringing his back feet forward. He puts the left one down first. As he thrusts himself forward with that foot, he rolls on to the diagonal right back/left front, with his neck and body more stretched. Then he leans forward on to his leading leg, while his back is bunching to bring his back legs forward. In the end he is flying again. As you will have realized, the difference between the canter and the gallop is that in the canter he puts the diagonal pair down together, whereas in the gallop he puts them down separately.

In this fairly fast canter the horse's head moves considerably backwards and forwards as he shortens and lengthens his back. Most horses find it difficult to canter more slowly unless

they have been helped by training, and if this is the case you may find it difficult to sit down at first. Your trouble is certainly tension, either in your back or your legs. If you hold on with your legs or try to support yourself in the stirrups, you will bounce worse. Losing your stirrups is a sign that you are clutching with your legs. You will feel more confident in the beginning if you put a strap round the horse's neck and hold it, leaning back slightly and pushing your navel towards the horse's ears.

Do not let yourself develop either of these common faults, which are seen even in experienced riders. One is pulling yourself down in the saddle by sitting too far back and holding on with your heels. You will get away with this on a sluggish horse, but anything more willing will run away with you. The other is rocking to and fro as if on a rocking horse, with your waist stiff. This upsets the horse's balance, making him clumsy and graceless.

If, instead of running, you canter like a horse, you will find that you can turn easily towards your leading leg but not away from it. A horse, too, leads on his inside leg when circling. If he is stiff on one side (many horses

are), he may try to use the same leg whichever way he is circling, or simply be very unwilling to canter one way. You can help him get more supple by using the exercises on pages 108 – 112, or by riding him over the bumpiest ground you can find.

You can tell which leg the horse is leading on when you are going in a straight line because you can feel his opposite hip thrust you forward first, followed by a slight roll towards the leading leg. Your hip on the leading side tends to be in front of the other one (try to feel it). If he wants to change legs while cantering, he will normally switch legs in mid-air (the flying change). Try to feel these changes through your spine so you do not have to lean forward over his shoulder to tell which leg he is leading on.

As with the walk and trot, the horse has different types of canter. Here he is in a relaxed, ordinary canter. In a collected canter he shortens his back, bunches himself up and tucks his nose in. Horses do not naturally do this as easily as they do a collected walk or trot. A collected canter is slower than a trot; a truly collected horse can canter as slowly as a man walking. Western horses are trained to canter

very slowly, but they sometimes lose all freedom of movement and start hobbling along, putting down each foot separately. This is not a true canter.

At an extended canter the horse lengthens his stride. As he goes faster, you feel a sudden jerk as he changes to a gallop. You can hear four footfalls, not three.

Here the outline of the rider's back has been superimposed on a photograph at a different stage of the stride so you can see how her supple back moves. The rise of the horse's loins and the thrust of his back legs throw you forward at each stride. If your back and legs are tight, you bounce. Leaning forward tightens your back so you bounce worse.

The gallop

In a gallop, the fastest pace of all, the horse's legs go down almost as in a canter but with the diagonal pair separated. You can hear four rapid hoofbeats, then a gap.

Here is the pony from page 10, this time with a rider. He is going very fast. He extends himself more in the middle of the stride than in a canter, and bunches himself up more as he draws his back legs forward. The forward thrust of his hips, and the rise and fall of his back, are also more pronounced.

Most people find it difficult, if not impossible, to sit to a gallop. By rising from the saddle, like this rider, you help yourself to absorb his movement: you also help the horse by allowing him to coil his back. The classical rider's stirrups are too long to allow him to do this, and he rarely gallops: the slightly shorter stirrups of the central seat were adopted for precisely this reason. The rider is securely balanced on her knee and heel; she drops her weight into her heel to keep her knee firm. Her bottom stays out of the saddle. She lets her hands move with his head movement.

If you compare these pictures with those of the same pony galloping by himself, you will see that his movements are identical although he is carrying some 15-20% of his bodyweight extra. He can only do this because his rider is well balanced and moving with him.

It is slightly more difficult to tell which leg the horse is leading on in a gallop, for you cannot feel it through your spine. But you can still feel the slight roll towards the leading leg, and you can feel that change when he shifts to the other leg. If the horse is stiff, he is likely to pull towards his leading leg, so he does not gallop in a straight line.

When a horse canters or gallops, he leads on the same leg behind as in front. Thus, if he is leading on the right front leg, his left feet, both back and front, go down before his right feet. Sometimes, though, he will change legs in front but not behind. This is called cantering (or galloping) 'disunited'. Here the pony is galloping disunited. He has paired his right back foot with his right front. As you can see, he looks extremely uncomfortable. If you were riding him, you would feel that something very wrong was happening. Compare this picture with the fifth picture in the sequence above and you will see the difference.

Usually the horse changes in front in the next stride so that he is moving properly; but if he does not, you should pull him up and start again, for he may hurt his back. It is usually young, stiff and unbalanced horses that canter disunited; but this pony is old, extremely supple and well balanced: he is merely fooling about and has jumped on to the wrong feet.

Uphill and downhill

In going up and down slopes, you still need to be balanced as if you were standing on your own feet. Your body will still be vertical, even if the horse's body is sloping up or down under you. So when he is going uphill you will be leaning forward relative to him, and when you are going downhill you will be leaning backward.

Going uphill, the rider here rises from the saddle, with her weight dropped well into her heel to keep her steady. Getting up off the horse's back lets him coil it under him so that his back legs can thrust powerfully forward. She puts her hands well forward, for he needs to stretch his neck more than usual.

Going up a steep or difficult bank, the horse is likely to rush and scramble. Your task is to leave him free to do it how he wants. The greatest danger is that you lose your balance, sit down suddenly so that he cannot move, and pull at the reins to keep yourself from sliding off. In that case, the horse will slither backward down the bank. To make sure this does not happen, take hold of a good chunk of mane halfway up his neck. Your hands will then move with his neck so that you cannot pull at the reins, and you will be less likely to lose your balance. Make sure you have come far enough forward, and that your weight is on your knees and heels. If you stand on your toes, you will push the stirrup backward so it slides off its holder.

If you are being led without reins, you should still put your hands forward, for it will help your balance. Even when you are more experienced, it is a good idea to rest your hands on the horse's neck, or not be too proud to hold his mane, when going up a difficult bank. The horse is likely to hop or bounce unexpectedly, and if you do not follow his movement but hurt and frighten him by pulling suddenly at the reins, he will develop a hatred of banks.

Use this position when you come to a ditch, too, and are tackling it slowly. When he jumps, the horse makes much the same movement as he does going over a bank. The trouble is that he usually stands and thinks first, then leaps rather unexpectedly. Some horses step over ditches while others leap them with miles to spare. If you are leaning forward and holding the mane halfway up, you will both arrive at the other side unhurt, whatever he chooses to do.

Going downhill, lean back a little but support yourself on the stirrups, with your heels well down. This takes the strain off the horse's back. If you sit right down on him, you make

his work more difficult. If you are going down a very steep slope, you will feel much safer at first if you push your feet forward, with your heels well down.

Leave your reins loose. The steeper the hill, the more you need to do this. In order to see the ground the horse needs to drop his head, which he cannot do if you are hanging on to the reins. If you have practised on steep slopes while being led, you will be quite comfortable with the idea of going downhill with nothing in front of you, but if you have not tackled them until you are riding with reins, the idea may scare you at first. But when you stop a horse from lowering his head, he is likely to fight you, to make you give him some rein, and you then may think that he wants to run away. Horses have more sense than to gallop down precipices, but they get very agitated if they cannot see when they know it is dangerous. Many horses also refuse to go down steep slopes if they feel you are not properly balanced. Trotting or

cantering downhill is far bumpier than on the flat, for the horse wiggles his hips more. Keeping your heels down will help you stay off his back so you are not bounced about.

Riding up and down slopes, especially steep ones, improves your seat far quicker than riding on the flat, and whenever you ride you will do well to take advantage of every bump you can find. You will also improve your horse's balance, suppleness and mental alertness, as well as his muscular development.

You may find that you are told to lean forward while going downhill. In the forward seat you do, but the conditions are usually rather different. The forward seat was developed for *fast* cross-country work. Banks are taken at a gallop; long downhill slopes are usually not very steep, and are also tackled fast. This is not beginner's work. Moreover, the forward-seat rider can only manage it by having his stirrups short and tucking his knees in behind the knee-rolls on the saddle.

How to practise sitting: on the lunge

When you first sit on a horse, your body, unused to its strange position, tends to crouch and stiffen. This is especially true if you are worried about controlling the horse. In your first lessons you should be free to think only about the way you sit, and about the feel of the horse's movement, until you feel confident and happy at any pace. Someone else controls the horse. There are various ways of doing this. If you are already a rider but want to improve, you will do best to go back to riding without reins, for only then can you concentrate fully on improving your seat. It cannot be stressed too often that the horse responds to your stiffness or lack of balance just as he responds to anything else you do.

Practising on the lunge

On the lunge, a long light rope or line, the horse moves in circles round his handler. The handler turns on the spot so that she is always facing the horse's middle, holding the lunge line in the hand facing the horse's head. If necessary, she uses a whip, flicking it behind him to keep him going or pointing it at his girth to stop him from wandering towards her. Otherwise, she controls him by voice, giving a series of brief tugs at the line when she wants him to slow down. Page 110 gives more details about lunging.

Learning how to lunge a horse to improve his movement is quite an art and takes special equipment, but learning to lunge to improve the rider is not so difficult. But if the horse is not used to it, remember that it is at first tiring and boring for him. Do not lunge him for more than 10 minutes in the beginning: reward him when he does well and stops when you ask; and remember to work him equally each way round.

Look at the photographs carefully, for the exact position of horse and lunger are

position. Leaning forward is the commonest beginner's mistake. Try to feel that your chest and stomach are open, not hunched up. Imagining that your navel is attached to the horse's ears with elastic is a good trick.

Make sure that you are not hanging on with your heels: if the horse rushes off, you are. If you find it difficult to relax your legs at a sitting trot, hold the front of the saddle, pull your bottom into the saddle with your shoulders back, and let your legs flop. Once you have relaxed, it is just as easy without holding on.

You can do all your exercises on a lunge rein. Another game is to ask your helper to name one of the horse's feet, then clap each time it touches the ground. Remember to keep your head high: if you look down, it changes your balance, and the shape of your spine.

You will also find it fun to ride without a saddle. Put a blanket over the horse's back, securing it with a long strap (a couple of stirrup leathers), for this spreads your weight better and makes him less slippy. Your position should be the same as when in the saddle. Let your legs hang long and your toes hang down. On a horse that moves steadily you will probably find it easier to sit down to a canter bareback. Make sure you are not sitting further back than in a saddle, or you will bounce. Riding without a saddle gets rid of your tension better than riding with one. You also get a delicious feeling of being really close to the horse, feeling his warmth and the muscles of his back.

In the Spanish Riding School in Vienna, where they train some of the best riders in the world, you would have daily lunge lessons for at least six months before being allowed any reins. Do aim for perfection. It is a great help to have someone take photographs or, better still, video you, so you can criticize your position.

Left, putting your hands behind your head keeps your shoulders back. This horse has a lunging cavesson with the line attached to the front. The whip drives him forward.

Above, by holding your arms forward at a trot, you can check how much you bounce. Holding your arms out keeps your shoulders back.

important. The lunge line is clipped to the back of a headcollar. Never lunge from the bit. One horse lunges well, so the handler is not using a whip: shaking the free end of the line at him is enough. If the horse fools about or tries to eat, put a bridle on him and tuck the reins behind the stirrup leathers. Make sure the outer rein does not pull his head outwards.

The riders are practising with their arms in different positions, sometimes with stirrups and sometimes without. If you are doing this, ask your lunger to pay careful attention to your

Vaulting: vaulting on and sitting

Vaulting (voltige) is a kind of ballet on horseback. It is a sport in its own right; it is also wonderful for developing a good seat and balance, a sense of rhythm and timing, and the feeling of joy, pride and fearlessness that any rider should know. It is great fun, too.

You will have to join a vaulting group: vaulting is not an at-home sport as it involves a team and special equipment. Cheap or makeshift surcingles should not be used as they may damage the horse's back.

Any riding group or school should be encouraged to train an instructor and a horse. The horse should be strong and steady: the longer his back, the more room there is for team work. He is lunged in extra-large circles to make his work and action easier. Most vaulting is done at a canter, with some practice at a walk; the horse never trots.

Gymnastic exercises are important in vaulting, for you must be fit and supple.

Vaulting on is not difficult if your timing is

This rider's back is stretched and supple. Holding her arms in this position helps keep her chest raised and her shoulders back without her stiffening. Her legs wrap softly round the horse; her toes point down, which prevents her gripping with her calves. This elegant and free-looking way of sitting is the basis of the central and classical seats.

right, for the horse's action swings you up. Canter beside him, leading on the same leg as he does, then grasp the handles and feel the rhythm of his canter. Your left hand clasps the handle from the front, knuckles up and fingers towards you, as if you were trying to punch yourself in the face. Your right hand holds the outer handle like a bicycle's. Your thumbs must lie *over* the handles or you will sprain them.

Canter for a couple more steps level with the surcingle, then jump forward on to both feet, landing in front of his shoulder. Spring up immediately, swinging your head down and your right leg up; your left leg should remain straight, toes pointed. The further in front of the surcingle you take off, the easier you will find it to land right behind it. Make your performance elegant, with straight legs, and land softly.

The surcingle helps keep your legs in the right position. Do not grip with them; lean back on your arms, sit right down, and relax. You will feel your back move with the horse's. This is far the easiest way to learn to sit to a canter: most people can do it the first time they try. When you are confident, raise your arms as shown, growing tall and proud.

The horse is ridden bareback, but with a thick protective pad. The surcingle is strengthened by a high-quality steel plate. It has large, angled handles and stirrup loops, and is well padded. The horse wears a bridle, side-reins and a cavesson. An extra-long lunge line and whip are needed.

Vaulting: some positions

Standing is considered elementary! Kneel behind the surcingle, then jump to your feet, landing lightly. The bend in your knees absorbs the movement of the horse's back.

Below, three members of a team work together to produce a harmonious and graceful picture. Arms and legs are always kept straight.

Once you feel confident cantering with your arms held out, you can choose from scores of other positions and exercises. These are all designed to help your riding in different ways: they supple your back, improve your leg or shoulder position, and develop your sense of balance, rhythm and timing.

Positions (static exercises) are held for four strides; movements (dynamic exercises), like scissors or somersaults along the horse's back, are timed so that the bounce of the horse's canter helps the swing of the movement.

Above, the young girl's handstand is steadied by an older vaulter. Acting as 'prop' tests the firmness of your seat. Teamwork and co-operation are particularly emphasized.

There are six basic exercises: sit, stand, flare (one version shown right), scissors, round the world – a complete 360° turn made by swinging the legs over the horse's back to sit sideways, backward, sideways and forward again – and flank, or dismount. Great attention is paid to the elegance and rhythm of the exercises, and the changes between them.

Anyone will benefit from vaulting, and the vaulting surcingle is of unique value in teaching the nervous, the handicapped, and others with learning difficulties.

In flare across the neck, the vaulter holds her arm and opposite leg high and straight. Flare along the back, facing forward, is one of the 'compulsory' exercises. If your back is not absorbing the horse's movement, your arm and leg bounce.

Competitive vaulting is mainly for the under-21s. Each vaulter must vault on and do the six basic exercises. He then does a *kur*, a sequence of exercises performed to music. As in skating, various types of exercises must be included: static, dynamic, one facing backward, one facing sideways, and so on. Marks are awarded for artistic impression as well as correctness and style.

In a team *kur*, the four or eight members of a team work together. The horse is never left empty but there may be one, two or three vaulters on board at any one time. The stronger members of the team may act as props for the younger or lighter ones, often in most spectacular ways.

Experienced vaulters usually work without hats, for they make some exercises difficult.

In scissors, the vaulter uses the bounce of the canter to help her swing her legs high. By turning her hips, she will land facing backward. She will reverse the move to turn forward again.

Being led

A third way of concentrating on your seat is to be led. This has advantages, too. You can tackle uneven or steep ground, which will help loosen your back so that you move as one with the horse. You can discover far more about his different ways of moving, turning and balancing himself than by riding in circles only. You can learn about your horse's character, about what startles him and what pleases him; about where he needs encouragement and

where he needs his head free so that he can peer at his footing. He in turn will enjoy going out, and will feel safer with someone at his head than being ridden by an unconfident rider. The disadvantages are that your helper cannot keep a constant eye on your position, and that you probably will not be able to canter. But if you can ride a sitting trot bareback, and scramble up and down banks, you will find cantering easy when the time comes.

Leading

A gentle pony can be led from a headcollar. Clip the lead rope to the back of the headcollar and hold it about half a metre from the horse's head. Hold the spare end loosely in your left hand but do not wrap it around your hand. If you hold a horse too tight when leading, he is likely to get worried as he cannot move his head freely to look about or help balance himself. But if you are going past something frightening, like a roadworks, hold him on a

Riding

Think about sitting tall, with your back free. Make sure you are sitting in the middle of the saddle, not on the back. Do not let your feet drift forward (a common fault). Check this by rising from the saddle from time to time, pushing your navel towards his ears. If you have to lean forward, it is because your feet are too far forward. Keep your weight in your heels and your toes forward, not out. Do not let yourself hold the saddle. You will need to hold his mane when he scrambles up a steep slope, but otherwise try to keep your hands free.

Ask your helper to use bumps and slopes, to change pace and stop, to go over ditches and under trees, and to be adventurous as he can. Try to feel through your spine what the horse is doing with his hips and back, and to recognize his different types of walk and trot. Practise your exercises, and practise riding bareback.

If the horse gets excited, or you are afraid, keep your bottom down in the saddle and your shoulders back. Make sure you are not clutching with your legs. If you sit calmly, it will help to calm him.

Like you, a horse works more willingly when his efforts are rewarded, so stroke and praise him when he does something difficult. Take note of what he pays attention to, and the way he moves his head to look at things, so that you learn how his mind works. This is one of the keys to good horsemanship. Riding is not only a matter of learning what to do with your body; you also need to understand the horse's likes and dislikes, his fears and ideas. You need to know how to keep calm and reassure him when he is scared, and how to recognize when he is being lazy. You will learn these better by being led out in open country than in many lessons on the lunge or in a school.

shorter rein and use your elbow and shoulder against his neck to stop him pushing against you. Speak calmly rather than angrily when he gets excited, and always praise him when he does well.

You can also lead from a bridle by taking the reins over the horse's head so that you have a decent length of lead. Take care not to be pulling at the bit or you will upset him and deaden his mouth.

The Second Principle
The horse is like a see-saw

A horse's weight is not carried equally by his front and back legs. Because of the weight of his head and neck, his front legs usually carry more weight than the back ones. By moving his head and neck back, he can put more weight further back, so it is more evenly balanced. He can throw his weight still further back by standing on his back legs or rearing. Or he can put more weight on his front legs by reaching his head and neck down and forward. His balance can tip forwards or backwards, like a see-saw. The middle of the see-saw, the balance point, is about where you sit.

Look at these horses playing, and you will see how their balance changes forwards and backwards, changing how they look.

You will have felt these changes of balance as you ride. When the horse is plodding along, head low, his see-saw is down in front. He feels heavy and dull. He is said to be 'heavy in front' or 'on the forehand'. Like a boat with too much weight in the front, he finds it difficult to change speed or direction. He wastes half his energy moving in this unbalanced, graceless way.

This horse has tipped his balance right back so that he is carrying all his weight on his back legs.

In slowing suddenly, this horse puts all his weight forward to bring his back legs under his body. A split second later he rocks backward and lifts his front end to swing round in a fast turn.

When he is moving briskly, his see-saw is balanced more evenly. His movements become lighter. He feels as if he could easily speed up or turn. When a horse is plodding along heavily and sees something that interests him, you can feel this change of balance dramatically. His whole front end lifts. If he is very excited, it feels as if he might even rise into the air like Pegasus, for his balance tips right back.

Clearly, since you are sitting on the balance point of his see-saw, your weight can tip his balance down in front or help to balance him evenly. So far we have stressed that you should be in perfect, upright balance all the time. But now you can find out how changing your balance changes his way of going.

Here he is turning as he walks. His head and neck are low, tipping his see-saw down in front, so he carries most of his weight on his front legs. He looks heavy and dull. When his balance is more even (left), he makes the turn more easily.

The horse's shape

The shape of the horse has a great effect on his natural balance. If he has a big, heavy head and neck, and small hindquarters, he will naturally tend to be heavy on the forehand. He will move heavily and clumsily unless he has special training to help him carry his balance more evenly. But as his hindquarters do more work, they will strengthen and get bigger, so his natural balance will improve, too.

The more a horse's neck springs up from his shoulder, rather than forward, the better his natural balance will be. In this respect the old classical breeds are superior to the more modern but bigger warmbloods. They find it easier to tip their balance right back, as is necessary for the advanced dressage movements such as *piaffe* (see page 122).

The horse above left is trotting slowly. His head and neck are low and stretched out so that his see-saw is down in front. He looks dull.

Above, he has pulled his head and neck up and back so that he is more evenly balanced. He looks livelier, although he is not going faster.

Your weight and the horse's balance

When you lean forwards or backwards, your weight affects the horse's see-saw. The rider in the sequence of photographs (below centre) is changing her pony's way of going by leaning forwards and backwards. Note that she is only changing her balance: she is not doing anything different with her hands, legs or back.

At first, the rider is deliberately leaning forward heavily (1.). Although this is a lively pony, she makes him plod along. His head is low and his neck stretched out. She has tipped his balance forward so he is heavy in front. He seems to find it hard going.

As she sits more upright (2.), his balance improves a little. His head lifts and his neck shortens. He is throwing more weight on to his back legs. To cope with this, his back shortens. At exactly the same point in his stride, he is having to put his back foot further forward underneath him to carry his weight.

When she sits straight (3.), his balance and way of going improve still more. He looks lively and bright, and is clearly carrying her more easily. He is using his back legs still

1.

The young horse's balance is naturally forward. Here the rider allows his balance to go with the horse's in an extended trot.

When the rider straightens up, the horse's balance lifts off his forehand, and he shortens his step.

more, and his head is higher and more pulled in.

When she starts to lean back (4.), his head comes up even further. The extra weight on his loins makes his work more difficult, and he is taking shorter steps with his back legs.

Leaning back more (5.) makes it impossible for him to coil his back under him and reach forward with his back feet. His balance is right back and he has almost stopped moving at all.

Imagine yourself carrying a large plank on

arch in the small of your back, so that it stiffens. You will already have found that this stops the horse from striding out freely.

You will also realize that leaning back slows and quietens the horse. This is extremely important, for it is unfortunately exactly the opposite of what you naturally do when you are afraid. Frightened human beings tend to crouch, leaning forward. If you are on a horse that is getting excited, or wanting to go faster than you

2. **3.** **4.** **5.**

your shoulder. When it tips down in front, you keep going; but your steps are heavy and your work is harder. When it tips down at the back, you lean back and slow down. When it is well balanced, you can turn, run, skip or stop with ease. You can see that this pony has the same difficulties when his rider unbalances him.

Experiment with these ideas on a quiet, relaxed horse. Do not move your legs, or tighten them, for that will make him respond in other ways too. Simply try to feel how he responds to your balance.

As a result, you should see that leaning forward makes the horse go heavily and clumsily. If you feel what it does to your back, you will also realize that you lose that springy

do, tensing up and crouching will only excite him further. What you must learn to do, unthinkingly and unhesitatingly, is to lean back with your legs loose. The only way you will change your natural reaction is with practise. So when you are on a lunge, or being led, make sure you lean back a little whenever the horse is slowing down, or when he is getting excited. Do not let fear clutch at your chest: keep your 'centre', that point just below your navel, down and open-feeling. Keep your shoulders open and back. As this becomes second nature, you will realize that by preventing yourself from showing your fear you also diminish the fear itself. Since horses are so sensitive to fear, you will also help calm the horse.

Rising and sitting

In the previous discussion you may have wondered why in the forward seat the rider seems to lean forward and yet this does not seem to make the horse go sluggishly.

On the left, the rider is shown in two positions in the forward seat: sitting and rising. A straight line through her body would show that, when she rises, she shifts her bottom and the upper part of her leg backward. Thus, although she is leaning forward, she is still in perfect balance. By rising she has not affected the horse's balance and way of going. But why has she done it?

1.

2.

Look at the pictures below. Here the rider is sitting down but with his stirrups short. This is sometimes called the 'light' seat. He is in good balance, with his heels under his hips. Incidentally, this is difficult to do with your stirrups short: most beginners who ride with short stirrups tend to sit on the back of the saddle in the unbalanced 'chair' seat. It is easier for you to sit well with longer stirrups.

The horse is cantering along slowly, not putting much effort into it. You can see that he is not really reaching forward under himself with his back feet, nor stretching out well with his front legs.

But when the rider rises from the saddle, 2., the horse immediately springs forward. Within a couple of strides he is using his back much more, coiling it under him and reaching further forward with his back feet so that he lengthens his stride. If you compare 2. with 7., you can see this clearly. Both photographs have caught the horse at the same point in his stride, when he is just about to touch down with his left hind foot. In 2. it is going to strike the ground about level with the back of the saddle. But in 7. it is much further forward. He has lengthened his stride, and speeded up.

Rising does not necessarily encourage the horse to go leaping forward. It merely allows him to if that is what he wants to do. If, like this horse, and cross-country jumpers, he is fit and keen, it will allow him to use himself to the full. This is why you see jumpers rising from the saddle throughout most of the course. But on a sluggish horse rising will have little effect.

Again you will see why it is important not to get tense when the horse wants to go faster than you do. When you tense your legs, you push your bottom out of the saddle, releasing his back so that he can spring forward. There will be times when you find this a grand trick, but as a beginner you probably do not want the horse to go leaping forward just because he is keen. So practise keeping your legs loose, your bottom down in the saddle and your shoulders back when your horse is keener than you are.

When you want to rise from the saddle, remember that you are not standing in the stirrups but putting your weight on your heels and knees, and rising off them.

4.   **5.**   **6.**   **7.**

In the racing and forward seats the rider usually rises to any canter or gallop, sitting only when he needs to push the horse on. But in the central and Western seats the rider rises only to the gallop. As well as making himself more comfortable, he is making the horse's work easier.

Leaning sideways

The horse does not simply see-saw forwards and backwards. In fact Baucher, one of the great writers on classical riding, said he is like a ball. You can roll him where you want. If you lean sideways, you will unbalance him sideways, and he will move to that side to put himself underneath you again.

The Western rider on the right is turning her horse by leaning sideways only. You can see that at first the horse is putting his head in the opposite direction to try to counterbalance what the rider is doing.

You can experiment with a quiet, relaxed horse to feel this effect. Take care that you are not leaning forward as well as sideways. If you push the front end of his see-saw down into the ground, he cannot swing it round so easily. If you actually lean back slightly, as well as sideways, you will tend to stop his back end, lightening his front end so it can swing round more sharply. This is the basis of the Western spin (page 146).

This way of using weight is used in Western riding and in polo. It is naturally used by any fast-moving rider who wants to turn sharply, whether he be an Australian sheep-herder, a Cossack, an Arab or a Mongolian. However, it is not used in classical riding. This is a question of style.

When a horse responds to this use of weight, he uses his head like this Western horse. It is perfectly natural for a horse to lean his body but not his head when he is turning fast, whether he is being ridden or not. A classically trained horse would do the same, as you will see if you watch one playing in a field. But in European riding great emphasis is placed on the horse bending round the curve, with his head leading the curve. This is not difficult since he is moving slowly. If the horse cannot

In classical riding the rider only turns his head and shoulders, thus **putting more weight on his seat bone on the side towards which he is turning.**

This Western rider is turning her horse by leaning sideways only. You can see that at first the horse puts his head in the opposite direction to try to counterbalance the rider's weight. Finding it does not work, he leans his own body and turns.

bend round a curve, but leans over like this horse, he cannot do the more difficult movements of higher training, for they depend on his body being supple.

In European riding, then, only a slight use of weight is usual. It is often referred to as 'putting pressure on one seat bone'. Looking at the rider on the left, you can see that her weight comes mostly on the right side of her bottom (or right seat bone) rather than squarely on both sides as it does when she is sitting upright. You can increase the pressure on your seat bone much more subtly by simply turning your head and shoulders in the direction you want to go. Try it when you are sitting on a hard chair. Without shifting your bottom, turn your head and shoulders to the left. You can feel the pressure on your left seat bone increase. When you are on the horse, all you need to do is to turn your head and shoulders in the direction you want to go, but keep your hips straight. Look at the classical rider on the far left. His hips are square with the horse's hips, but he turns his shoulders with the horse's.

Your horse may not seem to notice this slight pressure. If he has been ridden by beginners who sway around in the saddle, he will have learned to ignore it. You can teach him to become more sensitive by using your weight more obviously and rewarding him when he responds. Each time you try it, use the subtle way at first, turning your head and shoulders; then increase your weight until he responds. If you praise and reward him well, he will gradually become more sensitive. A horse that has always been ridden well, in perfect balance, responds to even the slightest shift of your head and shoulders. So do young horses. It is our careless riding that teaches a horse to lose his natural responsiveness.

THE THIRD PRINCIPLE
The horse reacts to pressure

If you unbalance a horse, or push and pull gently at him, he moves to take the pressure off and make himself comfortable, just as you would. Depending on where you put the pressure, he will move different parts of his body. Like you, he responds better when the pressure is put on gently but insistently. If you thump or yank, he will object and do the opposite of what you hope. Like yours, his sense organs respond to changes of pressure rather than pressure itself. A series of small nudges will move somebody over better than simply pushing harder and harder. Try experimenting with these ideas with a friend, human or horse.

The ways we ask a horse to respond are called the 'aids'. 'Aid' means 'help'. In fact the Duke of Newcastle in his famous book on equitation used the word 'helps', for they are ways that you help the horse to understand what you want him to do. He responds naturally when you offer your help in the right way. Even an 'untrained' horse does, as long as he is calm. But a tense or frightened horse, like a hysterical person, does not accept your help: he fights instead. When you start to experiment with the aids, remember that calmness comes first. You cannot help a horse if either of you is agitated or angry.

By sitting on the horse's back you obviously limit the number of places you can put pressure on a horse, although when you are handling him from the ground you will use a far greater range. Over the centuries people have discovered what helps horses accept most easily, and have built up systems of training to increase the horse's sensitivity to them. Some horses are naturally more sensitive than others; and different cultures, or different trainers, want their horses to move in different ways. So you will find that there is no 'right' amount of pressure to use: you have to feel how each individual horse responds, and modify what you do to get the results you want. Remember that you are not issuing orders, but trying to help the horse respond. Roughness seldom makes the horse respond more willingly. Horses that have been battered about rather than helped become sullen and insensitive. Try to avoid riding these ones (unfortunately they are often the ones offered to beginners), for they will only make you ride rudely and unhelpfully yourself.

As well as the five 'natural' aids – your weight, your back, your legs, your hands and your voice – there are also 'artificial' aids – whips and spurs. Both need using precisely and delicately. The novice rider's problem is usually that he is not using the natural aids precisely enough, so using whips or spurs is unlikely to improve his results.

This section shows how and why each aid works by itself. Once you have seen what a horse naturally does with his body in various movements, you can see how to use your aids together to ask him to do those movements.

Your *weight* affects the horse's balance and therefore his way of going. You have already found out how he responds (pages 50 – 54).

Your *back* encourages him to use his back and his back legs more.

Your *legs* affect his back legs.

Your *hands*, through the reins, act on his head, neck and shoulders.

Your *voice* can soothe, praise or frighten him. You can also train him to respond to certain words. Horses are quick to learn word commands but, like dogs, they need proper training and reward. Mostly their natural talent is not used to the full except in the circus. But they are also naturally responsive to the tone of our voices. If you scream 'whoa', even a well-trained horse is unlikely to stop, because the tone of your voice, with its urgent message of danger, is to him more important than the sound he has had to learn to recognize. If you want a horse to calm down or stop, speak calmly; if you want him to attend, speak sharply; if you want him to move faster, speak briskly.

Horses respond well to praise. In early training all horses are praised and rewarded at the same time, so they learn to connect the two. Later you will find that a horse works as well for praise as for reward.

Pushing with your back

Normally when you sit, your back has an arch, which this rider is deliberately exaggerating. When you push with it, the arch straightens out. You are then pushing the horse forward with your bottom or seat bones.

horse's movement to move the arch in your back, so that your back swings with his at every stride. Let your back be as free as possible. When you can feel his rhythm well, deliberately increase the swing so that you are actually pushing him forward each time he swings forward. He will then lengthen his stride. You will realize that if you lean forward there is no arch in your back anyway; so there is no swing, and the push does not work. In fact, you may find that putting your shoulders back makes it work better, for in this way you increase the arch in your back and thus the swing.

If you do this at a walk, you will ask for an extended walk. If you do it at a sitting trot, you will ask for an extended trot. At a canter, you will ask for an extended canter or gallop.

If you use a more sudden push, especially on

When you push with your back, the horse coils his back under him. His back rises, his rump drops, and his back feet reach further forward under him. If you use this aid by itself, then, he will take longer strides.

This is a subtle aid. If you over-use it, your arms tend to go stiff. Many people find the idea difficult to grasp at first, so it may take some experimenting before you can use it well. It is a little like the way you push with your bottom to make a swing go higher. But if you imagine doing that, you will realize that you cannot do it forcefully without stiffening your arms and legs. That, of course, would also affect the horse. You have to experiment to find out where to draw the line.

Try it first at a relaxed walk. Allow the

a well-balanced and active horse, he is more likely to go straight into a canter from whatever pace he is in.

You often see showjumpers pushing with their backs just before a jump, as on the right, below. The rider has sat down suddenly, pushing, asking the horse to get his hind legs under him for the take-off. You will also see less accomplished riders letting their arms stiffen so that they lose control of the reins. (You may even see this stiffening of the arms in dressage competitions, when the rider is asking for an extended trot: the effect is ugly and rigid-looking.) When using any of the aids, you should check that the efforts of one part of your body are not tensing or jerking another part.

You may find this called the 'seat aid'. Here it is called 'pushing with your back', firstly because that is what you actually do and secondly because the word 'seat' is used to mean different things. It can mean the way you sit; it can be a polite term for your bottom; or it can mean, as here, pushing with your back.

Another way to use your back is to brace it. Tip your shoulders slightly back and push your chest upwards. This gives you more of an arch in your back, while your back muscles are more active. This way of sitting, always used by the classical rider, has a more constant effect on the horse's way of going, tipping his see-saw backwards.

In your experiments to find the link between the way your back works and the effect on the horse, notice that if you just stiffen your back the horse no longer strides out so freely. He is stiffening his back too; since he no longer coils it under him so much, he takes shorter steps. His spine moves with yours. When yours is stiff, so is his; when yours is free, so is his; when yours is active, so is his.

Above, when the rider pushes with her back, the horse coils his back and extends his stride. His loins rise and his back foot reaches further forward.

Pushing with both legs

Pushing with both legs makes the horse use his back legs more actively, so he will go faster. If he were stung by a fly at the spot where you use your heel, he would kick at it with his back foot. By pushing there you ask for this response in a less violent way.

1. When the horse is standing, the rider's legs are relaxed.
2. When she pushes with both her legs, you can see the horse react.
3. She goes on pushing and the horse walks forward.
4. As soon as the horse is going, the rider relaxes her legs again.
5. She would only use her legs again if she wanted the horse to go faster.
6. This rider moves her legs from its usual position into the horse's side and pushes. Notice that her knee does not come away from the saddle.

If you run your finger quite firmly along the horse's side at about the level of your heel, you will find he twitches or flinches, and may even raise his back leg, when you are prodding just behind the girth. This is where you press your heel in. When you prod higher up he does not respond so much. If your legs are too short for the horse you are riding, you will not get such good responses out of him.

Since the horse accelerates when you press your heel in, you can now see why clutching with your legs is such a bad idea. If the horse is sensitive, he will run away with you. If he is not, he will get used to the constant pressure, so that you find it difficult to get him to respond.

If the horse does not respond, nudge at him insistently until he does. Avoid thumping and kicking: it only makes him sullen. Nudges work better.

Take care that you are not tightening all of

1.

2.

3.

4.

5.

6.

your leg. If you do this, you will push your bottom up out of the saddle. You will then not be able to use your back at the same time as your legs. In fact, you quite often do want to use both at the same time in asking the horse to go faster or change pace.

When the horse is walking, you can ask him to trot by squeezing hard, increasing your squeeze with nudges if you need to, until he trots . But if you simply nudge him briefly at every step, you will ask him to walk faster and more actively. You will get the best response when you use your legs alternately, but your timing must be good.

First, watch as a horse is led away from you with the stirrups swinging. Each stirrup hits the horse's side just before the leg on that side hits the ground. If you can time your squeeze like that, the horse will be in exactly the right position to push harder with his back leg as it goes down. Now try walking along on a bareback horse, with your legs swinging freely. If you let the horse's hips move your hips from side to side, rather than swinging them forwards and backwards, your legs will bump against the horse's sides exactly as the stirrups do. Turn the bump into a nudge and the horse will walk more actively. Two more points should become clear while you are working with this idea. First, it is not a good idea to leave the stirrups hanging while you lead a horse about, as they are likely to nudge him into going faster. Second, the more you have thought about feeling when the horse is putting his foot down, and which foot, the easier you will find it to get the timing exactly right.

To keep an active trot while rising to the trot, squeeze with both legs as you sit down. At a canter, squeeze just as he is about to push his back foot down after he has been airborne.

Pushing with one leg

This horse is standing still. When his rider puts his right leg back slightly and pushes with it, the horse steps away, to the left, with his back legs. His front end stays still, so his head comes round to the right.

When you put your heel back slightly and push with it, the horse moves his hindquarters sideways, away from the pressure.

Go back to standing beside the horse and prodding at his side with a forefinger. As you move your finger back from the point where your heel acts to ask him to go forward, you will find you come to a point where, instead of twitching or flinching, he moves his hindquarters away from you. Probably he will do this by picking up the hind leg on your side, putting it down under the middle of his body, then swinging his weight on to it so he pushes his hindquarters away from you and your prodding finger. The best way to ask him to do that when riding is to put your heel back a hand's breadth, then push.

Try pushing with one leg while the horse is standing still. If he is a horse that has been ridden by muddled people, he may think that you too are muddled and you really want him to go forward. If he is facing a gate, or someone is at his head, your meaning will be clearer. A well-ridden horse (or a young one) will move away from your leg straight away. You may even be able to turn him right round, leaving his front legs in the same place.

Try pushing with one leg while you are moving too. A good place to try this is when you are walking down the middle of a lane. When you push with your right leg, the horse gradually shifts over to the left side of the lane. Again you may find that a horse that has been badly ridden will think you mean him to go faster, but a well-ridden horse will shift over well. He will not bend his body in the direction you are going, but will keep it straight or even let his front legs lag behind his back ones.

You will find that the horse shifts over better if you time your push to arrive when he is about

to put his back leg – in this case the right one – down. He will then move it over to the left before he steps on it. You can feel this moment because his right hip starts to drop as he lowers his foot. You will find this difficult to feel unless your back is stretched and supple.

If you use your inside leg when you are riding on the lunge, the horse will swing his hindquarters out so they make a bigger circle than his front legs. He will then move half-sideways, his head pulled in by the lunge line. If, on the other hand, you use your outside leg, you will stop his hindquarters from drifting out. Since again his head is restrained, his body will bend so that it curves round the circle he is on. If he is stiff, he will not want to bend but will simply move inwards. In that case, use your inside leg in the 'move forward' position, on the girth, to drive him out to his original circle.

When you play about with these ideas on different horses, you will notice that some move away from the leg better than others. They all do it well, at first; but many people do not ask them to do it, so they lose their sensitivity. You can help your horse regain his sensitivity by praising him when he does well.

This horse is moving forward strongly. When his rider pushes with his right leg, the horse moves his hindquarters to the left. You can see his right back leg going across to the left under his body. But since he is also pushing forward with his back legs, his front end tends to move across too, so that his whole body moves to the left.

Holding and using the reins

Hold the reins gently in your fists, across the palms of your hands. Your fingers, wrists and arms should be soft, supple and relaxed.

Of all the aids, your hands are the most likely to give you and the horse trouble if you use them badly. Roughly handled, any bit can be painful. When he is afraid of pain, the horse will tense himself up, fight, or become dull and insensitive, depending on his character. Whichever way he chooses to react, it will not help in creating a harmonious partnership. So before you pick up the reins, look at what is in your horse's mouth and think about how it must feel. A horse's mouth is no less sensitive than yours. (On pages 148 – 153 you can learn about the different kinds of bit and how they work.)

Never pull on the reins. You can use them in three ways. You can let your hands move with the horse's head, so there is no pressure on the reins and he moves freely (giving). You can stop them moving, so that he cannot stretch his head or front legs forward freely (resisting). Or you can move them sideways or upwards to

move his head and neck (asking). When you ask with the rein, or stop your hand, you may need to give a series of little squeezes with your fist, as if you were squeezing a ball or milking a cow, just as you sometimes need to give a series of nudges with your legs when the horse does not immediately take notice of your asking. But you do not ever pull a rein towards you, or put a steady pressure on it, or jerk at it by using your whole arm, for these encourage the horse to fight you or push against the rein instead of giving when you ask.

Practise first in an enclosed space or while on the lunge, so that if you lose control you do not panic and use the reins too harshly. Hold the reins in your fists, with your arms and shoulders soft and relaxed. There should be a straight line between your elbows and the horse's mouth: if your wrists turn in or out, or if your arms are tight so that your hands come up, your touch on the reins will be stiff and unkind. Relax your arms, and especially your wrists, and your touch will be kind.

There should be no pressure on the rein until you squeeze it by tightening your fist. When you squeeze, it should feel as if you have caught a little fish. Shorten or lengthen your reins until this is true when your hands are each side of the front of the saddle.

At a standstill, play with this little fish. If the horse's head and jaw are relaxed, he will nod his head at your squeezes (see pages 148 and 150). If he feels dead, keep playing until he relaxes. Horses that have been ridden badly do deaden themselves to avoid being hurt, and they need to be played with until they relax. Do not pull the reins: that will make the horse tense

against you. Any time you ride, have patience and play with your reins until you feel that he is relaxed and listening to you.

When the horse moves, let your hands move with his head so the reins do not tighten at every step. You will find that at a trot his head is higher and stiller than at a walk.

Do not keep a constant pressure on the rein. When the horse is relaxed, he can feel the changes in your hand best when the rein is almost slack. By keeping a constant tight hold you only deaden his mouth, so you have less control, not more. Unfortunately this point is widely misunderstood. If your hands are not 'light' – soft, gentle and kind – you will never ride well. The greatest damage is caused by riders with rough hands.

The horse's head moves to and fro as he steps forward. Let your arms swing from the shoulder so that your hands move too, or the reins will tighten at every step.

When you stop your hands moving, the horse cannot stretch his head forward, so he cannot step forward freely. Squeeze your fists so the reins do not slip through them.

The open rein

When you move your hand out to one side, the horse turns his head towards that side, just as he does when you are leading him.

Usually you only need to move your hand a few centimetres. On a young horse you may need to move it further; on a well-trained horse you really only need to turn your shoulders, and your hand will move enough for the horse to feel it through the rein.

Notice that this only asks the horse to turn his head, not the rest of him. He can, of course, walk, trot, or even gallop straight forward with his head turned to one side. If he is standing still, he will turn his head, but he will not move: it is your legs that ask him to move (see pages 84 – 89 for standstill turns).

Beginners often believe that you 'steer' a horse with your reins. It is an idea that comes naturally to us: most of the time we do control things with our hands. Unfortunately, though, like crouching forward when you are afraid, this instinct is totally out of place on a horse. You can turn a horse's head with your rein; but the rest of him will not turn unless he happens to want to go that way. Take your time to experiment quietly and slowly until you can teach yourself that your instinct is wrong, or you will find that you do the wrong thing when you are excited.

You may find that the horse stiffens his jaw and refuses to respond to you. Do not simply pull at him, for he will just pull back. Instead, squeeze the rein again and again with your fist so that he relaxes his jaw and turns his head. If he seems particularly obnoxious about it, keep calm. Work with him at a standstill until he turns his head for you, and praise him for it. Then go back to trying it on the move.

You use your open rein like this in European-style riding when you are asking the horse to turn. You always want him to bend his whole body round the curve, with his head and neck turned in the direction he is going. You will, of course, be turning your shoulders a little, so that your weight goes slightly more on to your seat bone on the side you are turning towards (see page 54). This will mean that your hand naturally comes back a little, as well as out. This little bit does not matter; but do not pull the rein deliberately back towards you. It has a quite different effect on the horse.

In the fast, leaning turns done in Western riding or polo, it does not matter where the horse puts his head. In fact, the faster he turns, the more likely he is to keep his head upright or even turned in the opposite direction. He needs to do this to keep his balance. In this type of riding, then, the open rein is hardly ever used except in a horse's early training.

Shorten each rein by sliding your hand up it like this. Always keep both reins the same length. If your horse walks with his head turned to one side, you are probably riding with that rein tighter than the other.

The horse turns his head and neck towards the open rein. Notice that this sensitive horse does not need to be pulled; nor does he need a bit.

The open rein from above. When the rider puts her hand to the left, the horse turns his head towards it.

The indirect rein

By moving your hand towards the horse's neck, you press the rein against his neck and shoulder, asking him to move them away from the pressure. On the right, the right indirect rein is being used. You can see that the horse has swayed his shoulders over to the left, but with his head straight.

This is called the 'indirect' rein because you use it on the opposite side to the way you want the horse to move. There is no pressure on the bit: the horse is reacting to the feel of the rein against his neck.

It is important that you do not cross your hand over his neck. If you do, you will start to put pressure on the bit, asking him to move his head to the right but his neck and shoulder to the left.

When you use the indirect rein at a standstill, the horse will probably not actually move away from it, although you will feel him shift his weight over to the opposite side. Unless the horse tips his see-saw backward, he is carrying too much weight on his front legs to move them without moving his back legs too. He will find it easier to respond when he is moving forward.

You often use this and the open rein at the same time, asking the horse to move his head, neck and shoulder in the same direction. This is easy to do if you use the slight shift of weight too, turning your head and shoulders in the direction you want to go. If your hands stay the same distance apart when you turn, you will automatically use the indirect rein. You also use it automatically if you ride with both your reins in the same hand.

Many beginners lean forward anxiously when they are trying to turn a horse. However, a moment's thought will tell you that the horse will then be carrying so much of his weight on his front legs that he will be much more difficult to manoeuvre. Leaning forward makes a rider have to use far too much pressure on the reins in order to get a response. When you are trying to feel how this aid works, remind yourself not to lean forward as you use the rein.

Many British riders never use an indirect rein, so their horses come to take no notice of it. However, a horse that does not respond to it cannot be asked to move his front end sideways, which is a handy thing to be able to do.

A second way of using your indirect rein is to move your hand upwards. This is never necessary on a well-trained horse. But if you are teaching an obstreperous horse to be more co-operative, it is a useful help. When a horse does not want to respond to your open rein, he sets his jaw, stiffens his neck and refuses to turn his head. Putting more pressure on the open rein usually makes him worse: he may even stick his head in the air. If you raise your opposite hand, the rein will press against his neck about halfway up. In response he will drop his neck and head towards your open rein.

You can thus use your indirect rein to persuade the horse to listen to your open rein. As you will see if you try it, the exact position of your rein is what the horse is responding to. If you put your hand high, the rein presses on the upper half of his neck, so he drops his neck and moves it away. If you use it lower and further back, as in the usual use of the indirect rein, it presses on the join of his neck and shoulder. He then moves his neck and shoulder to the side. By changing the position of your rein, you can ask for exactly the response you want.

As the rein touches his right shoulder lightly, the horse moves away from it. There is no pressure on the bit. The rider's hand does not cross the horse's neck.

The neck rein

A Western horse carries his head low, so that the rider can throw a rope forward without hitting the horse's head. He usually wears a curb bit or hackamore, so that the end of the rein is below and behind his mouth. The rider carries his hand high because of the saddlehorn. A European horse, by comparison, carries his head higher; the rein ends more or less at his mouth; the rider's hands are lower. The point at which the rein crosses his neck is therefore quite different, and the response not so easily produced.

Here the horse moves his neck and shoulder away from the rein laid against his neck. The neck rein is the Western development of the indirect rein. It is also often used in polo or any sport where the rider has both reins in one hand and turns fast.

A Western horse comes to respond to the lightest touch of the rein on his neck. Notice that he does not bend his head in the direction he is turning. Helped by the rider's weight, he leans into the turn with his head straight. He turns like a bicycle; a European-style horse keeps his body upright and bends round the curve, like a tricycle. Both ways of turning are natural to a horse. The one used is a question of style, and also of what is appropriate for the work the horse has to do.

You may find that some horses do not respond well. This may be because their natural response has not been rewarded and sharpened. But it may also be because the angle of the rein, and thus the point at which it touches the neck, are different in the different styles of riding.

It is difficult to use a neck rein with a snaffle bit without touching the bit and confusing the horse. If you want to experiment with getting this response from a horse that is not usually ridden with a neck rein, you will do better to

ride without a bit. He will respond most easily in a bosal (page 152), which is what Western horses often use in training. If you do not have one, put your reins on the *back* ring of a head-collar. The reins then have more contact with his neck, and you can use them more strongly until his response improves without fear of confusing him by pulling on a bit. However, he may be more difficult to stop in a headcollar, so try this only in a small enclosed space while he is in a quiet mood. Praise him when he responds well and he will improve. Once he has realized you want this response, you will be able to put him back in a bit; but make sure your rein is loose when you neck rein.

Although neck reining is not in the purist school of European riding, it is extremely useful. It means you can ride one-handed, and turn fast. It used to be considered part of the education of any 'bridle-wise' horse, that is, a horse that responds sensitively to a rein wherever it is placed.

Since the horse moves his shoulder sideways away from the neck rein, it is particularly important not to lean forward and tip his balance on to his front legs. Thus the slightly backward seat often used by the cowboy helps the horse in this response.

70

The rider puts her hand to the left, the direction she wants to turn. The horse turns his front end away from the rein.

Here the horse is turning right. He has no bridle, so you can see he is responding only to the rein against his neck. When a bit is used, the rein is loose.

71

How the horse changes speed

You have now discovered how to affect the position of the horse's head, neck, shoulders and back legs. You can tilt his balance forward, backward or sideways. You can ask him to use his back and his back legs more actively. The next step is to see exactly what a horse does with his body when he makes a particular movement. You can then understand what combination of aids to use when you want him to make that movement.

Watch your horse playing in a field, trying to see what he does with his legs and his balance. He often moves so fast that it is difficult to tell what he is doing. These pictures catch the horses in mid-movement, while they are changing speed.

When you are riding on a lunge or being led, try to feel the changes in balance shown here, as the horse goes faster or slower. You will find that he slows down more tidily when you lean back, for you are helping him.

The horse on the left is slowing from a trot to a walk. He has tipped his weight backward, bringing his back legs forward under his body and tucking his nose in.

The horse on the left has stopped suddenly from mid-gallop, so the changes in his body are more obvious than if he were stopping from a walk. He has thrown his weight backward

This horse is speeding up. There are various ways he can go faster when he is trotting. Here he has chosen to make his strides longer, going from an ordinary trot into an extended trot. He has dropped his hindquarters as he coils his back and reaches as far forward as possible with his back foot. You can see the great push of his hindquarters as he surges forward with immense strides.

so that he is almost sitting. He has pulled his head in to help shift his balance. To support his weight, he has brought his back feet forward by coiling his back.

The horse on the left has chosen to go from a trot straight into a gallop. Again he tips his weight back for a second, pulling his nose in to help rebalance himself. He drops his hindquarters to coil his back and bring his back legs forward under him to support his weight. Meanwhile, he has lifted his front legs right off the ground to reorganize them for a canter stride. He then springs forward powerfully, already in a fair gallop, tipping his weight forward again as he reaches forward with his head and front legs.

You can see that he needs to throw his weight back and stand on his back legs for a split second in order to get both his front legs off the ground together. In a trot one is down while the other is up; in a gallop they both move forward more or less together. But the backward tilt only lasts for long enough for him to raise his front legs; after that his balance goes back to normal. In contrast, when he is slowing down or stopping, his weight stays back until he has finished slowing.

73

Slowing and stopping

Ideally, the horse stops willingly whenever you want. He stops with his feet square, his back bunched up and his back legs under him. He does not raise his head as he stops but pulls it in. This is considered a perfect stop because he is then in a position to spring off again in any direction or pace you want.

However, horses sometimes do not want to stop. Your main worry at first is bound to be whether you can stop at all, let alone perfectly. Moreover, it is actually quite difficult to achieve a perfect stop. It is difficult to judge how much leg to use, because this varies enormously according to the horse's keenness, his response to the bit and so on. You need some experience before you can judge this.

For the beginner, then, the easiest and most certain way to stop is to lean back, pushing your bottom firmly down into the saddle, and stop your hands moving. Clench your fists round the reins, with your thumbs over the top to stop

them slipping. You do not need to pull. It is your *weight* that stops him more than your hand. A horse can, if he wants, set his jaw against the bit and still charge off with you. But he cannot charge off if you are tipping his see-saw backward, no matter how rude a horse he is. You need to use your weight.

Stopping in this manner is not elegant. The horse may throw his head in the air. He may drop his back under you, so that his back legs are spread-eagled out behind. This is not particularly good for his back. But he will stop. Once you know you can stop, start aiming for perfect stops. Do not lean back so far, but merely put your shoulders back. Push with your back so that your bottom pushes down in the saddle. Close your legs slightly, not exactly pushing with your heels but just beginning to touch his sides. Watch his head. It comes up when he dips his back under you. If you are pushing forward, it will not come up. Think of

When you want to stop, lean back a little, push slightly with your legs and back, and stop your hands moving. This stop is crude but effective.

When a horse stops, he puts his weight back, his back legs under him, and tucks in his nose. Below, the same ridden perfectly.

driving him into a wall: your firm hands.

A good stop is more comfortable for a horse. If you make him uncomfortable as he stops, he will not like the idea of it. Some horses will not stop because they are frightened of the bit: when they feel pressure on the bit, they stiffen against it and rush off. This is usually because people have yanked at the reins and hurt them. Changing the bit often helps. If the horse gets excited every time you use the rein, either your hands are too rough or the bit is too savage. It sounds contradictory, but a horse that is hard to stop in a harsh bit is often easier in a gentler one. This is because his natural reaction to pain or fear is to run away. If you remove the cause of the fear, he no longer wants to run.

There are other causes for a horse running away with you. Old riding-school horses, whose mouths are deadened by years of abuse, may take off simply to get home faster. Use your weight; turning the horse in a circle often helps.

He may be overfed, especially with concentrated food, so that he is bursting with energy. He may also be reacting to your tension, which frightens him. Keeping your shoulders back, your bottom down and your legs loose will calm him.

Do not be put off by this catalogue of possible disasters. Most horses stop willingly when you use the right aids, and all stop eventually if you use your weight. Unfortunately, though, too many novices have been terrified by being carried off because they did not know how to stop. As you have seen, it takes time before you can control your natural reactions to fear: leaning forward, clutching with your legs, and jerking at the reins. All of these drive the horse on. Practise in safe circumstances until keeping your bottom down and your weight back become second nature. Then you will be safe: you will enjoy your riding, and ride the better for it.

Going faster

A horse has several ways of going faster. He can take quicker steps. He can take longer strides. Or he can change to a pace that allows him to go faster. He cannot walk as fast as he can trot, nor trot as fast as he can canter, although he *can* trot or canter as slowly as he walks. A gallop is the fastest pace, and cannot be done slowly.

The rider above is going from trot to canter. This is the change of pace that most novices find most difficult.

When the free horse (see below) wanted to canter from a trot, he coiled his back, reached right forward with his back legs, tipped his weight back so he was standing on his back legs and lifted his front legs off the ground to rearrange them. Then he tipped his weight forward again as he reached forward with his front legs.

What our rider does, then, is to sit down and push with her back to coil the horse's back; she pushes with her legs to activate his back legs; she tips her shoulders back to help him rebalance; and she stops her hand momentarily so he tucks his nose in. His front legs then come up instead of reaching forward. She does this all

forward more positively. Instead of closing her legs gently on the horse's sides, she is giving a distinct sharp nudge; and instead of pressing her bottom down, she is giving a real swing forward with her back.

At a trot, if you use your legs only, the horse will trot quicker. You are not asking him to canter, merely to use his back legs more briskly.

When you ask for a canter in this way, the horse will lead on whichever leg he prefers. If you want to ask him to lead on a particular leg, you will have to combine these aids with those for turning (see next page and page 85). He leads on the leg he is turning towards.

Other ways of going faster

From a standstill to a walk: push with both legs, making sure your hand is free.

For a faster walk: use your legs briefly at each stride, or use each leg alternately as described on page 60.

For longer strides at the walk: use your back to push at every stride, as well as your legs.

From walk to trot: squeeze with both legs, and keep squeezing until he trots. Some horses need a nudge or several nudges. Avoid kicking: it deadens a horse's sides. If you think you need to kick, you have not yet found how to use your legs properly. You may be jerking the reins every time you use your legs, too.

For a faster trot: use your legs at every stride.

For an extended trot: sit down and use your seat and legs at every stride. Check his speed until you can feel his back rise under you. Then let your hands go forward. The horse puts his head down and forward, to match his forward-reaching front legs, so your reins need to lengthen.

For a gallop from a canter: push hard with your seat and legs, then rise from the saddle.

at the same time, for a split second. Next moment, feeling the horse change pace, she releases her hand so he can reach forward with his front legs, and she sits more upright so he can put his weight on them.

These appear to be almost the same aids as for a stop, so you may wonder why the horse does not stop. If you compare the photographs of the horse stopping on page 72 with this one striking off into a canter, you will see that they are doing very similar things with their bodies. The difference is that the horse that has stopped has his front feet planted on the ground; but his balance, back, back legs and head are still like the other horse's. It is not surprising that the aids are similar. The differences are in timing and in the strength of the aids. In asking for a canter the rider only applies the aids for a moment; next moment she has released her hand and changed her balance. And she is using her back and legs much more strongly when asking for the canter, so the horse is driven

How the horse changes direction

As you watch horses playing, you will see that they have many different ways of changing direction. Often they will switch from one to another in mid-turn. They can use several ways of turning at a standstill, and several while moving. They can also move sideways.

Turning fast and sharply, he throws his weight into the turn, like a bicycle. His head is upright, not leading the turn. By using it as a counterbalance, he can lean his body further and turn more sharply. His weight is back and his back legs are right underneath him; he lifts his front end and throws it on one side. This is the way Western horses are encouraged to turn.

Above, the horse is turning on the spot. His weight is forward on his front legs, which move on the same spot while he moves his back end round them. This is a rather untidy version of a turn on the forehand.

A supple horse can also move sideways, by taking sideways steps and crossing his legs. He keeps his body straight. He will move at any angle he chooses.

With different combinations of the aids, you can ask the horse to turn any way you want, as he does naturally. But what you need to do at first is to work at a simple turn until you and the horse are working harmoniously together. Gradually you will master one after the other until you can switch from one to the other at speed, as he does himself. But do notice especially how the horse's balance changes in the turns. If you are not supple and well balanced, he will not be able to make even simple turns without your wrestling with him. For the wonderfully gymnastic exercises this horse is doing he needs to be supple, agile and well balanced. Even then he cannot do them with your weight on him unless you are, too.

Below, another turn on the spot. This time he has put his back legs under his body, leaned back on to them and is moving his front end round. This is a turn on the haunches.

Turning slowly, (above) his whole body bends in a smooth curve, with his head leading. He does not lean his body over, but takes longer steps with his outside (here right) legs than with the inside ones. He steers himself round the corner like a tricycle. This is a classic moving turn.

79

The moving turn: European-style

Here you can see how the rider slides her outside leg back behind the girth, to push the horse's hindquarters to the left. Her inside leg is in the normal position.

You want the horse to bend his body in a smooth curve, with his head leading the bend. If you want to circle to the left from a straight line, you will want the horse's head to go left, his shoulder to go left and his hindquarters to go left.

This rider is turning left. She turns the horse's head by using her open rein. She turns his shoulder with her indirect rein. She turns his hindquarters by using her right leg behind the girth. Her two legs are therefore in different positions. She has turned her own shoulders with the horse's but kept her hips straight, so she has put more pressure on her left seat bone. It may also be necessary to push with the left leg on the girth in the 'keep moving' position.

There are a number of common beginner's mistakes. One is to lean forward anxiously, making the horse's front end heavier and more difficult to turn. The straighter you sit and the more you use your legs, the easier the horse will turn. Aim at using your hands as little as possible, and use your legs before your hands.

Using only one rein in the hope that the horse will follow his head is a slovenly practice that will not always work, since a horse can still move, at all speeds, with his head turned to one side. It is your *legs* that turn his body.

Pulling the inside rein towards you does not have the same effect as an open rein. In fact, it makes the horse's hindquarters swing out so he does not bend round the curve. Use an open rein. Never pull a rein.

There are various ways in which the horse may try to avoid doing what you ask. He may set his jaw and refuse to turn his head towards your open rein. Do not increase the pressure, but play with the rein with repeated squeezes of your hand. If he sticks his head in the air,

raise your outside hand so he drops his neck, turning it towards your inside rein.

He may be so stiff that he cannot bend his body easily. He will then try to keep his body straight by turning his shoulder in too much. It feels as if his front end is slithering sideways, and it is called 'falling in on the shoulder'. In this case do not use any indirect rein. Increase the pressure with your inside leg. You can then feel that your inside leg is like a pillar and you are bending the horse round it. The more you use your legs, the more you will get his body to bend.

Some riding-school horses try to cheat by making the circle smaller. If yours does, use your inside leg strongly to drive him forward, adding a back push at every stride. If you are trotting, you will have to sit down. If the horse is moving actively, he will find it easier to make a large circle than a small one. Do not turn his head outwards: if you do, he will simply go in small circles with his head turned outwards, which is not the point of the exercise.

As you can see, you often have to experiment with the balance of your aids until you get the exact response you want. This is perfectly normal: all horses feel different. If you have always ridden the same horse and have therefore found the combination that he responds to best, do not be angry when another horse fails to respond in the same way. Horses do not know what is 'right'; they respond to what you are doing. If they do not understand your language, it is no use shouting it louder. Go back to basics: find out how the horse responds to each aid and then find the combination that works for that horse. Once you have found it, try to make your aids lighter, so that your riding is pleasanter for the horse, and he will respond more willingly.

Moving in a curve: Western-style

You want the horse to move as he naturally does in a fast turn. He leans over like a bicycle rather than bending his body round the curve.

This rider guides the horse's front end into the turn with her neck rein. She leans his body sideways by using her weight. She uses her outside leg behind the girth to stop his hindquarters from sliding out too far.

At first you will not be turning as quickly or sharply as this; but your aids will be the same even on a slow, gentle turn. If the horse does not respond to your neck rein, put your hand higher and further up his neck, like this rider, rather than bringing it further across your body. If you move your hand too far, the rein will start to pull on the bit. By putting your hand forward you lay the rein on a more responsive part of his neck without affecting his mouth.

It is physically impossible for a horse to bend his body round a curve as sharp as this at speed: his backbone does not bend enough. (On page 109 you can see how far a supple horse can bend sideways.) Even if you ride European-style, you will have to use this type of turn if you play fast games such as polo, horseball or gymkhana games, or if you want to herd cattle or sheep. The faster and sharper the turn, the more you will have to leave the horse's head alone so that he can use it as a counterbalance if necessary: hence the use of the neck rein, which positions his neck but not his head.

Practise slow turns until you are working smoothly and harmoniously. If you use your rein too sharply (a common beginner's mistake), the horse is liable to tense his neck and throw his head up. When he does this, he dips his back. Look again at the pictures on page 51. When the rider was leaning backward, the horse's head went up and his back dipped. Although his reasons for doing it were different,

the effect was that his back legs were pushed
out behind him. He was unable to bring his
back feet forward under his body, so he took
smaller and smaller steps, and he slowed down.
If the horse throws his head up when you are
trying to make a fast turn, you will find that he
suddenly loses power. So make sure that your
horse's head stays low on slow turns before you
start trying to speed up.

In all your riding you will find that it is
impossible to make progress unless you attend
to details, even in simple, slow manoeuvres. At
a higher level mistakes become exaggerated.
Aim for a feeling of real smoothness and
harmony at a walk before speeding up.

When you use your weight in a turn like
this, do not slide about in the saddle. Your hips
should stay square, like this rider's. Barrel-
racers, who make the fastest, sharpest turns of
this type, often steady themselves by holding
the horn with one hand so they do not slither
to one side and disturb the horse's balance.

The standstill turn

In a decent-sized space you seldom need to turn round on the spot. You can go forward and make a small half-circle, using your moving turn. In a riding school you are unlikely to be asked to turn round on the spot. But if you go the wrong way up a narrow track while out riding in the country, you will have to.

Inexperienced riders usually try to turn their horses round at a standstill by using the same aids as for a moving turn. A moment's thought will tell you that this cannot possibly work, for you would be asking the horse to coil his whole body into a knot, putting his tail in his mouth. He cannot.

Think carefully about how he turns at a standstill. He can, as you have seen, do it in various ways. He can leave his front legs in the same place and walk his back legs round them (turn on the forehand). He can leave his back legs in the same place and walk his front legs round them (turn on the haunches). Or he can move his front legs one way and his back legs the other way, so the middle of him stays in the same place. Try playing with a matchbox, or a model horse, and you will understand. Horses are not very bendy.

This last turn, swivelling the horse round so that you, on his middle, stay in the same place, is the easiest and most practical for you to learn at first.

From above, you can see that to turn anti-clockwise at a standstill you want the horse's head to go left, his shoulders to go left, but his hindquarters to go right. Therefore, what the rider is doing is using her left leg behind the girth to push his hindquarters right. She starts with this aid because it is easier for the horse to move his back legs first. She uses her left rein as an open rein to turn his head left, and uses her right rein as an indirect rein, bringing it

against the shoulder so the horse turns his shoulder left.

Do not lean forward or you make the turn more difficult for the horse. If he does not move, keep nudging with your left leg behind the girth until he does. Once his back legs are active, he will be able to move the front ones. As a rule, if you fail to make any movement you are not using your legs enough.

When you turn like this, you are not asking the horse to move his legs in any particular way: as long as he turns round and goes in the opposite direction that is all you want. There is not a perfect way of doing it, except easily and smoothly. For that reason it is not regarded as a pure movement, like the turn on the forehand or the turn on the haunches. These are used to develop delicate and precise control. There is little point in doing them unless you do them accurately, for they serve as foundations for higher training, and foundations need to be accurate. This turn, then, is simply for early practical use in a tight spot. As you and your horse improve, try perfecting the other two.

At a standstill, turn by using your leg and open rein on the same side. If he does not turn, use more leg, not more hand.

The turn on the forehand

forward, make sure you are using your leg in the right place, well behind the girth. It is worth getting off and prodding his side to find his most sensitive spot, for the nerve endings are in different places in different types of horse. Praise him when he responds, then try again mounted. This is a natural response, but one that horses may lose through being ridden badly.

Notice that this is a different use of your inside rein. You are not asking the horse to turn his head and neck; in fact your steady right hand prevents that. What you are asking is that the horse tip his head: nothing more. But this use of the rein also affects his hindquarters. Since he cannot move his front towards the rein, he takes the pressure off by moving his hindquarters in the opposite direction, to the right. This rein then asks for the same action as your leg, making it easier for the horse to step round with his back legs.

On a sensitive horse you can feel the effect of this rein alone. Face a gate or wall. Keep your right hand still; ask with your left rein, with repeated squeezes. Use both legs gently at the girth so you are asking him to move. He may step backward; but he will also step to the right with his hindquarters.

Think about the effect of this rein. You will now see more clearly why, in turning a circle, you always use your inside rein as an open rein. If you pull it towards you (a common fault), you push the horse's hindquarters out. Since you are pushing them in with your outside leg, this is clearly nonsense, and the horse will be the first to notice and resent it.

Finish this turn by urging the horse to walk smartly away. During the turn he tends to put his weight forward to move his back end more easily. Walking briskly away will bring his balance back so that it is more even.

Here the horse turns his hindquarters round his front legs. He does not swivel on his front legs: his front feet rise and fall in the same rhythm as his back feet. The inside front foot rises on the same spot, while the outside one makes a small circle round it.

This turn is used to improve the horse's response to your leg pushing his hindquarters away. It also improves his suppleness, for he has to reach forward and sideways with his inside back leg. It is useful for opening a gate without getting off since you can move the horse's hindquarters round the open end of the gate as you are holding it. In this case it will not matter so much if you are leaning forward as you hold the gate because it is the horse's back legs that are doing the work.

Practise this turn especially on a horse that does not move away from your leg well. If he persists in thinking you want him to move

From above, you can see that the horse is turning his hindquarters to the right. His head is tipped very slightly to the left, but his neck is straight. The rider is using her left leg strongly behind the girth. Her right hand is steady, keeping the horse from moving forward. Her left hand squeezes and releases the rein, but it does not move outward. She is not using an open rein, for she does not want the horse's head to turn.

The turn on the haunches

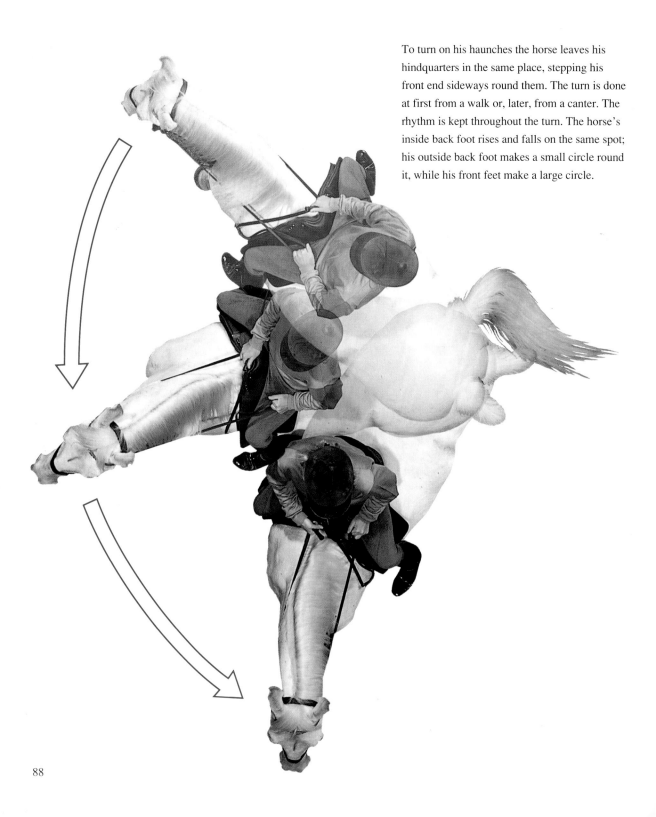

To turn on his haunches the horse leaves his hindquarters in the same place, stepping his front end sideways round them. The turn is done at first from a walk or, later, from a canter. The rhythm is kept throughout the turn. The horse's inside back foot rises and falls on the same spot; his outside back foot makes a small circle round it, while his front feet make a large circle.

You cannot do this turn unless the horse has learned to rebalance himself so that his weight is mostly on his back legs. Nor can you do it on a horse that does not respond to your indirect rein. It is used as an exercise to develop and test his balance, activity and responsiveness.

Here, on the left, the horse is turning anti-clockwise. The rider is using a slight open rein (left) and her indirect rein (right) to move the horse's front end over. Her hands are almost stopped, not allowing the horse to step forward. Her weight is tipped slightly to the rear, to help the horse tip his balance backward. This means that she can also use her back to push the horse's back legs forward underneath him. She turns her shoulder with the horse's shoulder, so she is using her left seat bone. She uses her right leg behind the girth to keep the horse's hindquarters in, and her left leg on the girth to keep him active. The horse's body is then bent in a smooth curve in the direction he is turning.

The Western version of this turn (right) is the pivot. The horse leaves his inner back leg on the same spot and swivels round it. The rider is using her neck rein; her legs are as the European rider's. Notice that she is not using her weight: she wants the horse to bend his body, not lean over.

This is fairly advanced work as it needs a well-balanced horse. Like other training movements, you will find it easier to understand the feeling if you try it first on a well-trained horse. It feels delightful if done well, since the horse is so light in front.

You will find it easiest if you walk the horse straight along a wall towards a corner. As you are about to hit the corner, slow down, put your shoulders back and ask the horse to

move his front end round, keeping his back legs active with your back and legs. The wall reminds him not to move his hindquarters.

You can also do this by walking in smaller and smaller circles, gradually tipping the horse's weight back and asking for more movement from his front, until he is making only a very small circle with his back legs.

You will not, however, have any success with this turn until you understand how to help the horse rebalance himself, for which you will have to have done some of the work described under the Fourth Principle, especially the half-halt (page 104).

The pivot is used a great deal in Western riding. It is only when the horse understands how to swivel round on his back legs that he can do the exciting faster turns.

Backing

Going backward is not easy for a horse: he seldom does it naturally, and finds it more difficult with your weight on board. Many horses have been forced backward with fierce pulling at the reins, so their mouths and backs have been hurt. Such horses hate to back, and must be asked in a way that is easy for them.

To back easily, the horse must have his hind legs under his body. He cannot step backward on to a leg that is stuck out behind his body. Many riders do not understand how to use their legs in stopping, so their horses stop badly and cannot then go backward. He must have come to a good square halt, with his back legs under him. You will have to encourage him to arch his neck and tuck his nose in, so that his back

can rise and he can step backward. If you are too forceful, he will stiffen his neck and raise his head instead, so go gently.

Do not try to back a horse until his head is in the right position. If his head and neck are raised, with his nose stuck out, his back will be dipped under you. You can feel that. He then cannot get his hind legs under his body: they will be strung out behind. In that position he will either refuse to back or will hurt his back in doing so.

If he refuses to nod to your squeezes, but stiffens his jaw instead, do ground work with him. Stand beside him with one hand on his nose; hold both the reins behind his jaw with the other hand. Now when you squeeze the

When he nods freely, squeeze the rein and keep it squeezed, with your hand still. Now use both your legs. You are asking him to use his back legs; you are telling him he cannot step forward. Logically he must step backward. Do not do more than three or four steps, then ask him to walk forward briskly by keeping your legs active and releasing your hand.

reins, push gently at his nose until he nods. Praise him. Do this again and again until he will nod to the rein pressure. If he will then do it when you are on his back, you may succeed in getting him to back.

If he still refuses to back, try backing him on the ground by pushing his nose towards his chest, or by pushing at his chest, or by pointing a whip at his front feet while holding the reins behind his jaw. Teach him to back when he is told 'back'. Use the word as well as the aids when you are mounted. When a horse has been hurt or frightened by being backed roughly, it will take calm training and kindness before he loses his fear. Having battles with him will only increase his tension and fear.

Before you ask the horse to back, play with the reins, squeezing and releasing them until the horse nods in response to your squeezes. You will feel his back rise under you when he nods.

Practising control: work in the school

Begin riding with reins while on the lunge or being led until you have got the feel of letting your hands move lightly with the horse's mouth. Keeping your reins the right length is important. When they are right, you can feel the horse's mouth when you squeeze or stop your hand, but not otherwise. You do not need a tight rein or a feeling of weight at the other end of it. Just as a dog will twist and turn with you on a slack lead, so a horse can feel the movement of your hand through the rein. If you ride with a constant weight on the rein, his mouth becomes deadened and he feels the change less sensitively. So keep your feel on the rein light, your shoulders and wrists relaxed and supple.

Stay on a long lead until you are sure you can stop. At a standstill, feel what your open rein does, and how to push the horse's hindquarters over with your leg. Experiment until you find what the horse responds to best.

When you start riding by yourself, use a school, that is, an enclosed space. Preferably it should be flat. A standard schooling arena is 20 metres by 40 metres, but if you cannot find an area that large do not worry. What does matter is that it is enclosed, for it will help the horse to be calm and concentrate on what you are doing.

It is also important that you do not use the field the horse lives in. To him his field is full of special places, resting spots, rolling spots, and places where you feed or release him. His feelings about these spots will distract him. He may, for instance, keep rushing to the gate. If you only have one field, barricade off one of the corners.

At first you will only need to change and control your speed, and change direction using your moving turn. Try to feel how your aids are affecting the horse. If he does not do what you think you are asking, the chances are that you are doing something wrong.

Keep the horse's pace brisk so that he always feels as if he is going somewhere, not just trudging about. This will improve his balance. As you both improve, try to use your aids increasingly lightly; do not get into the habit of using strong aids just because you needed them at first, when you were unco-ordinated and he unbalanced. Keep checking that you are not leaning forward and your legs are not drifting forward.

School work usually starts with a bit of brisk walking and trotting to warm the horse up. But endless trotting in circles will do neither of you much good. You can use the figures shown, or any others you make up (see also page 102). Try to make your changes of pace crisp, and to perfect good halts. It is in the changes, either of direction or pace, that you both benefit most.

When you start to canter, you will have to tell the horse which leg to lead on. He normally leads with his inside leg on a circle, so to ask him to lead on, say, his left leg you combine the cantering aids (page 76) with those for going left. That is, use your left open rein and right leg behind the girth (a tap works best), as well as the push with your back and slight stopping of your hand. This is easiest to do going into a corner. If he always canters on the same leg, he is stiff on one side. Supple him by trotting in circles towards the leg he dislikes. This will gradually loosen him up, but only if you bend his body round the curve (see page 108).

When you canter in a figure-of-eight, change legs as you cross the middle to circle the other way. Drop to a trot for a pace or two, then start cantering again on the other leg.

Finish your schooling session by letting the horse stroll about, relaxed, on a loose rein, while you make a fuss of him.

1.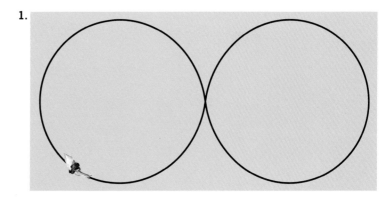

2.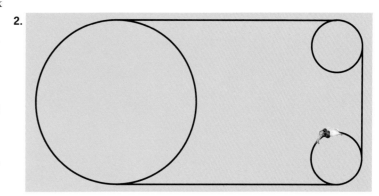

3.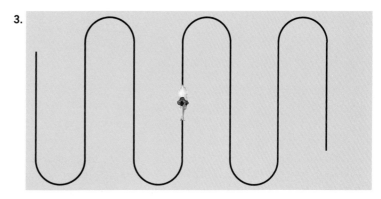

1. Make your figure-of-eight with round loops, bending the horse's body in a smooth curve.

2. Circles and voltes (6 metres across) supple the horse's body. Do voltes at a slow, sitting trot.

3. A serpentine up the school. Keep a steady rhythm throughout all these figures.

Hacking

When you start riding round the countryside, you will probably find your horse quite different. He is more alert. His movements are livelier and freer. Sometimes he pays more attention to his surroundings than to you. He may be startled sometimes. He may have fairly definite ideas about where he should go, and how fast. But unless he has been ridden roughly or unsympathetically he will enjoy himself, and show you much more of his true character.

At first you are safer riding with someone else. Horses like company and are likely to copy each other. If one feels confident in his rider, the second will see that there is nothing to fear. But you should also try to build up your horse's confidence in you. He has been taught to think of you as his leader, so try to show the characteristics of a good leader. Be calm and clear; do not dither about or let him take over. If he does not want to do what you have asked, do not get angry but simply go on insisting, quite calmly, until he does. Do not give up for a second. He will soon learn to respect you. Do not be rough, just insistent.

A horse is very sensitive to nervousness in his rider. He tends to assume you must have seen something terrifying, and he would be better off somewhere else. If you feel him getting nervous, stop him, calm him down and rub his neck. When they are frightened, horses tense up their necks and mouths so the reins have little effect. Rubbing their necks takes the tension away. If he has seen something that worries him, keep his head towards it, and try to be relaxed and cheerful, even laughing at his silliness. He will feel that you are not afraid, and his fear will die down. If you really are afraid and do not think you can act otherwise, you may be better getting off and walking for a while. It is a good idea to push to your limits of

confidence, but it is not a good idea to ride a horse that frightens you. It will make you ride badly, and may lead to disaster. Change the horse, or ride him only in places where you feel safe until you gain more confidence.

As you start to work together better in a partnership, get more ambitious. Do not always go the same ways; turn him off paths, up banks or round trees, so you keep him interested and alert. Horses do get bored. The more different situations you can master together, the better your partnership will become.

You can 'school' a horse just as well out hacking as in a school, so do not think that hacking is lazy. Do not let him plod along drearily. Keep him moving actively, with your rein light, so his balance is more even. This may be hard work at first, but as his muscles develop it will become a habit. Do not always do the same things in the same places or the horse will become quite fixed-minded about them. In particular, do not always gallop in the same place, for the day will come when you find you cannot do anything else.

Try to avoid riding on roads. Horses do not mix well with traffic. Even if the horse is reliable, drivers may not be. If you have to use the road, go quietly, never faster than a controlled trot. If you are with someone else, ride side by side, with the calmest horse nearest the traffic. Use hand signals like a car driver, and do not be afraid to ask drivers to slow down. Take special care at junctions. Be careful about grass verges: they often conceal broken bottles or other trash. It is never safe to gallop along a verge, for the horse may leap out in front of the traffic.

A horse can never feel happy or go freely if you hang on to his mouth. As far as possible try to use your back, weight and legs.

THE FOURTH PRINCIPLE
The horse's power comes from behind

The horse's main power is in the great muscles of his rump. He has far more muscle there than in his shoulders. It is his back legs, rather than his front legs, that drive him forward.

When he is plodding along with his see-saw tipped down in front, he is using his power to push himself forward in rather an inefficient way. Think of pushing along a plank with its front end on the ground. You waste half your energy. But when the horse wants to change speed or direction quickly, his balance alters dramatically. His weight goes back, he drops his bottom nearer the ground and he reaches further forward underneath his body with his back legs. He has done the equivalent of your picking up the plank and carrying it on your shoulder. It is a much more efficient use of power.

Watch horses playing fast games and you will see that, each time they want to use their power to the full, they rebalance themselves and bring their back legs forward under them.

A horse that really wants to make the best use of his power always shifts his balance backward and puts his back legs further forward under him to support his weight. But look what

The horse below keeps his balance back as he coils his back and draws his back feet forward under his body. He can then launch himself powerfully forward.

He drops his rump and brings his hind leg forward under him in this superbly athletic sideways move.

In turning from a gallop, the horse first tips forward with his neck stretched out so that he can reach forward with his back legs. He plants his back feet under his middle, throws his weight back on to them and whirls his front end round. In a split second he has leaped off in a full gallop again.

Try doing the same thing with your back sagging. You simply cannot get your knees forward. Your back has to rise.

By tucking his nose in the horse helps to take more of his weight off his front end. When his head is stuck out, it tips his balance forward. But note that this is a different, separate action. The rise of the back and the pulling in of the nose are not necessarily connected. For instance, in an extended trot the horse raises his back and brings his hind feet further forward at each step (see page 72). But his head and neck are still stretched out. In contrast, he can pull his nose in so that his neck is arched while still dipping his back and leaving his back legs strung out behind him. Many Arabs tend to do this. But when he raises his back and tucks his nose in, he rebalances himself and uses his power to the full. He does that naturally, whenever he wants to manoeuvre himself fast.

happens to the rest of his body. His back shortens and rises as he drops his rump. He pulls his nose in so that his neck arches.

Try this yourself, kneeling on all fours. Move forward with your knees towards your hands. Your back will lift as your hips go down and forward. You will now find it much easier to lift your hands off the ground. Like the horse moving his back legs forward, you have been able to carry more weight on your knees and rebalance yourself.

Changing the horse's balance to use his power

The basis of higher training is to use the horse's power, his side of the partnership, to the full. You will find that this is not mere exploitation on your part: you will have to contribute your gifts, your patience, understanding, and intelligence, to the full, too. You have seen that, whenever the horse wants to maximize his power and agility, he rebalances himself and carries himself in a particular way. He shortens his back, drops his rump, and carries more of his weight on his back legs. You can ask and help the horse to do this, not just for a split second when he wants to, but for an increasing amount of the time. His power is then always at the ready, on tap whenever you want. You can manoeuvre him as fast and easily as your own body. To ride such a horse is a delight. You seem to dance together.

When you rebalance a horse properly, he becomes far more sensitive to the aids, since you put him in a position where he is able to respond to them easily. You can teach any horse to carry himself well, though obviously some have more talent for it than others. Some are simply unable to reach a very high standard because of physical difficulties. A horse with weak hocks or loins will never be able to do what this horse (a Lusitano) can do. But far more of them are clumsy and graceless because they have never been shown how to use their bodies. A heavy cob, for example, usually has poor natural balance, tending to tip his see-saw well forward. But his loins and hocks are usually strong and able to cope with this type of work. By teaching him to rebalance himself, you can change the feel of him beyond all recognition, until he, too, feels as light as a dancing partner. You will find, as well, that the horse actually enjoys the feeling as much as you do: he becomes more playful and lively.

The horse above is trotting normally. The horse's back is long. His head and neck are stuck out in front. His weight is mostly on his front legs. Notice that his back foot does not reach far forward under him. He is just pushing himself along from behind. From this position he would have difficulty changing pace or direction. He would make the movement clumsily, or would take a second to rebalance himself before he could do so. A horse that always moves like this wears out his front shoes faster than his back ones, for they carry more weight.

If you were to sit on this horse in *passage*, you would be astonished at the feeling of power and energy under you. But see how calm he is. The explosive force he has developed would be positively alarming, and even dangerous, if that were not so. The rider is demanding a good deal of effort from the horse. But he does so with such calmness, patience and tact that the horse is never resentful or angry. You cannot bully a horse into this work. The more you demand from him, the more you must make use of your own gifts.

Below, the rider has rebalanced the horse and asked him to use his back legs more actively, so they carry more of his weight. The rider is doing this by using his legs and back more. But he is stopping the horse from going faster by not giving so much with the reins. The horse then tucks his nose in, so his balance shifts to the rear. Notice that the rider is not pulling at the reins, or putting a dead weight on them. He merely asks the horse not to reach forward, by stopping his hand a little. This requires delicate use of the reins. This is a 'collected' trot, so-called because the horse looks as if he has pulled himself together. His steps are shorter and higher. A horse that habitually moves like this wears his back shoes out before his front ones.

Above, the rider has asked the horse for even more active use of his back legs, and to shift his balance backward even more. But he is still not allowing the horse to go faster: in fact he is going slower, but his increased power makes him spring higher. This elegant, prancing pace is the *passage*. Notice that the rider is not hauling the horse's weight backward, but using his back to ask the horse to coil his. The superimposed outline from the image on the far left shows that the horse's back is now much shorter; he has dropped his rump; and he is bending his leg joints much more.

Feeling the power

It is extremely difficult for you to know when you have helped the horse rebalance himself, and got the full use of his power, unless you know what it feels like. By far the best way is to ride a highly trained horse that knows his work.

If you have the opportunity, seize it. If you have a balanced seat, relaxed legs and a light touch on the rein, you have nothing to fear from such a horse. He will be far more sensitive than other horses. Crude, rough, unbalanced riding will upset him. Ridden properly, he can teach you within five minutes the exhilaration of being on a calm, controllable but great force. Once you have felt it, you are unlikely to be satisfied with riding anything less.

Start by riding the horse quite relaxed. Gradually, tip your shoulders slightly back so you can use your back better to push him forward. Start squeezing (carefully) with your legs. The horse's head will come up and he will move more briskly. Shorten your reins to allow for the amount his head has risen, and control

your speed by stopping your hand, playing with the reins with little squeezes. You will feel the horse change his balance like the horse on the previous page, but you must keep pushing him forward with your back and legs. When you hit the right combination of aids, he will suddenly feel twice the horse. His steps become prancier; his back rises under you; and you find that he is instantly manoeuvrable.

If you have not this opportunity, learn to recognize the points at which he naturally collects himself. As you have seen, he probably does it when playing in his field. But he will also have done it with you on his back, whether you asked for it or not.

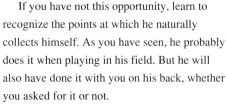

The first thing to recognize is the feeling of the horse's back rising under you as he brings his hind legs forward under him. This happens as he leaps forward in a racing start. It happens when he backs well, and especially in the moment when you release your hand and ask him to go briskly forward; when he bounces straight into a trot from an active walk; when he sees something in the hedge and trots by with a high, active trot; when he pulls back and wheels away from another horse that has threatened him; when he bounces through deep water. It will happen to you again and again. You can feel it better bareback, like this rider.

The horse's back also rises when he does an extended trot, but here he stretches his head, neck and front legs forward. However, his back legs are still reaching well forward under his body. An extended trot is used as a way of encouraging him to use his hind leg power to the full, although his balance is still to the front.

This horse is using his loins powerfully, dropping his rump and using his hocks well. His rider has got his full power in forward movement; she could now use her back to rebalance him, and her hand to remind him not to go so fast. He would then do *passage*, like the horse on page 99.

You cannot rebalance a horse by pulling the reins. You can (and people do) pull the reins so the horse's nose is dragged in and his neck arches, and then tell yourself he is the 'right shape'. You can (and people do) use various mechanical devices to force him into the 'right shape'. But it has absolutely no effect on his back legs. Moreover, taking a firm grip on the reins while driving the horse forward does not encourage him to rebalance himself: it merely allows him to remain heavy in front since you obligingly carry the weight of his head for him. The whole point of the exercise, which is to teach the horse to put his balance further back and his back legs underneath him, is lost.

When you have learned to recognize the moments when your horse naturally rebalances himself, you can try to prolong them: keep your shoulders back so you can use your back well, keep pushing him on with your legs and, with little light squeezes of the rein, let him know that he is not to speed up.

Using turns to rebalance the horse

How are you to rebalance the horse and maximize his power? If you truly know the feel of what you are aiming for, you simply ask and help the horse, using your balance to shift his balance, your back to get him to coil his back so it rises under you, your legs to keep his legs active and your hand to remind him gently not to go faster. But it is hard work for the horse, and he is likely to resent it if he does not see the point.

It is as well, then, to start by asking the horse to make the sort of manoeuvres that he cannot do unless his hind legs are under him and his balance is shifted to the rear. You can use the school, or find moments and situations while out hacking. By building up these exercises and moments, you will gradually build up his

strength and fitness. He will need to develop his muscles differently before he can hold himself well for an hour at a time: his hindquarters must grow stronger, while his neck may take on a permanent arch. Over months of training he will change shape considerably.

If you have always ridden the horse in brisk, active paces on a light rein, you will have prepared him well. He only uses his back legs well in true free forward movement.

One simple exercise is to ask the horse to use his back legs properly and then make tight, fast turns. He cannot do this unless he shifts his balance to the rear. If you have got his back legs active to start with, he will be able to do this more easily.

In the picture above the rider is using cones

strongly at the reins. This he resents, raising his nose, so that his back drops and his back legs cannot reach under him.

When she helps him rebalance by putting her shoulders back, she can also use her back more strongly to ask him to coil his back. He tips his weight back and brings his hind legs under him. In this position he can suddenly dance nimbly in and out of the cones. He is not going any slower, but you can see how much easier he finds it. You can also see that she is now barely having to use her hands at all to turn him, for in this position he is more responsive to lighter aids.

You can do this exercise while out hacking, too, using trees or bushes. Remember to get a good trot before you start the turns, and use your legs throughout so that the horse does not stop using his back legs actively. Do not let the horse lean on your hands: if you find him taking a hold, give repeated squeezes on the reins. This, and your own balance, will help him shift his balance backward.

When you experiment with this exercise, you will soon find that you get no results on a sluggish horse. If the horse does not develop full power with his back legs, he cannot shift his weight back on them, or will grind to a halt when he tries. He will develop full power most naturally if you make sure that he always moves forward freely. When out hacking, ask him to stride out well at every pace. He should always feel as if he is going somewhere positively, even at a walk. Ask him to trot or canter uphill; work him over banks; keep him lively; and make sure you are not putting a dead weight on his mouth. At first it may be hard work for you, but he will gradually develop the habit of always moving forward freely. Only then will you be able to find out what he can do with his power when you rebalance him.

that she has dotted at random around the field. The horse will be more interested in a game than in merely being worked hard, and his interest will in itself help him hold himself well.

First she trots him round the outside of the school, using her back and legs strongly until he is doing a lively, active trot. The more active he is, the better. Then she turns suddenly, weaving him in and out of the cones in unexpected patterns. She keeps using her legs, so his back legs keep working hard. When she tries tight turns, she finds she is going at them so fast she can hardly get round them.

At first (right) she deliberately does not help him rebalance himself. The result, as you can see, is horrible. With his balance down in front, she cannot turn his front end except by hauling

Changes of pace and half-halts

Other moments when the horse naturally rebalances himself and brings his hind feet further forward are when he changes pace or stops suddenly. It is in making swift changes that he uses his power best. You can use these moments as exercises, too.

Above, on the right, the rider is changing from walk to trot. The horse is relaxed, and has to shuffle for a couple of paces while he shortens his back and gets his back legs under him. Only then can he make the change, but when he does so his balance is good. He would have to do the same thing when slowing. So the rider asks him to change pace every few strides, say every six or ten. He soon finds that it is easier to stay in good balance, with his hind legs under him, all the time.

For this exercise to work, your changes of pace must be crisp. At first they will not be; but as the horse uses himself better, they come crisper. Pay special attention to the downward changes. If you are not using your legs and back to push the horse's hind legs under him, he will slow down with a dipped back and his hind legs out behind him. If you cannot do a perfect halt from a walk, you will not do a good downward change from trot to walk; so perfect your halts first. Watch the horse's head particularly. If he raises it when you halt or change pace, he is not using his back well, but dipping it.

Try to feel what he is doing with his back, too. You should feel it rise under you. When he is moving well, it will stay risen and round under you all the time. It should feel elastic, not stiff. His paces, too, will change. They become bouncier and softer, as if he were on a rubber floor. If you have been too rough with your aids, especially your hands, he will tense his back and his steps will feel stiffer, not freer. Aim at producing a dancer, not a clockwork toy.

If you were to carry this exercise to its logical conclusion, you would arrive at the point where you were asking for a change in pace at every step. If you have felt the horse's back properly, you will realize that what makes him rebalance himself is not the change itself but his *preparation* for the change. So, if you ask him for a downward change and then, before he has had time to make it, ask him to go forward as before, he will still rebalance himself.

This exercise, the half-halt, is shown on the right below. The rider uses his back and legs to ask for more power; prevents the horse from using that power to go forward faster; uses his shoulders to ask the horse to tip his balance back on to his well-placed, active back legs. Again this is not a matter of hauling at the reins: it is his back and back legs you have to influence.

Do not try to do too much in one half-halt:

you will probably need to do a series of them, quite subtly, to rebalance the horse. As you move forward from the half-halt do not give so much with your hands that he can stretch his neck forward and drop on to his forehand again. This is a question of delicate rein control, and of using your legs. Use a half-halt before any exercise that requires good balance, such as a turn on the haunches.

A third simple exercise is to ask the horse to back a couple of steps, then trot forward immediately. You will find these exercises more successful if you use a more classical seat, pushing your chest forward and up. Try this movement when you are sitting on a chair: you will feel your back muscles brace. This helps keep the horse's back active; but it will not work if you are too far back in the saddle. If the back of the saddle is low, try putting a soft pad under it.

Evasions

When a horse is truly rebalanced, he responds to changes in your hand through the weight of an almost slack rein: you can see that from earlier photographs. He can be ridden with a piece of thread instead of a rein, for he does not resist it. He is then said to be 'on the bit'. This is a confusing term (it did not originate in English) for it seems to mean you should feel a weight in your hand. You should not: the jaw and poll should be so relaxed that you feel nothing, though his head and neck move. In fact, if he is pushing on the bit he is not well balanced, but is using the bit to lean on. He is avoiding the effort of carrying himself well, letting you do the work for him. When he is on the bit he needs no support.

Once a horse is strong and educated enough to carry himself well, he is likely to enjoy his new-found sense of power and become more lively and playful. But, like any gymnastic exercise, it is hard work at first. If his back and back legs are not strong enough, he cannot put his weight back on to them; if your hands are heavy, he will lean on them, or will try to escape them altogether. Here are two common ways of escaping.

On the right, he is said to be 'behind the bit'. He has pulled his nose in and down too far, rocking his weight on to his front legs. When a horse does this, he feels as if he were trying to dig a hole, not go forward. Because of the loss of forward movement you suddenly have no control, as if in a boat with its sails flapping. This happens when the rider uses her hands too strongly, trying to pull the horse's head in. If he does not have the strength to push himself against a strong rein, or his mouth is sensitive, this is what he will do. Note that he is not bending at the poll, but further back, half way down his neck.

You should be able to see how to correct this (centre): use your back to make him use his, use your legs to drive him forward, and release your hand. His head will come up as he is pushed forward. After a few strides, control your speed by playing with the reins in gentle squeezes, but not a steady pull.

On the right, the horse is said to be 'above the bit'. He has dipped his back so his hind legs are out behind him. This is of course exactly the reverse of what you want. Moreover, tipping his head up makes the pressure on the bit come at a different angle: a snaffle bit will no longer act on the bars of the mouth but on the corners, having less effect (see page 148).

Horses do this for two main reasons. Firstly, a horse with a sensitive mouth will go above the bit when the bit, or the rider's hands, are too harsh. Changing the bit for a softer one, and taking care with your hands, will help. Secondly, if the horse is too weak in the back or hocks for the work he is being asked to do, he will not be able to raise his back and use his back legs more powerfully. He needs to be strengthened with work in extended paces on a longer rein. Although his balance is still forward in an extended pace, he raises his back and reaches forward with his back legs, using both to the full. When they are stronger, they will be able to carry the extra weight that is thrown on them when he is rebalanced. Making him work hard up hills also strengthens his back and back legs.

Some horses go above the bit simply because their early education was bad. A young horse will naturally stiffen his neck and jaw when pressure is put on the bit. A good trainer with tactful hands coaxes the horse to relax so that he nods his head, bending at the poll and slackening his lower jaw. A bad trainer increases the steady pressure until the horse tips his head up to avoid it. This soon becomes a habit. Retrain such a horse with patience and tactful hands, remembering that any horse will bend at the poll if you offer him a reward behind his chin. You do not need any mechanical devices: in fact they often confuse

the work, since you can train a horse to hold his head in the 'right' position without affecting his balance or how he is using his rear end. Use the horse's head position as an indication that all is well behind, but no more than that.

It should also be obvious that strapping the horse's jaw shut with a noseband will not help him relax his jaw and accept the bit.

Straight and supple: the volte

Another common difficulty arises when the horse is stiff. He has to be supple in his back to reach his hind legs forward under his body. Equally common is the problem that he is stiffer on one side than the other. Most horses are stiffer on the left. This is partly natural, but is helped by the fact that we almost always lead them from the left, asking the right side to bend and supple. The horse can then swing his left hind foot well forward, but not his right one. If you watch a horse being led away from you, you will notice that he often moves his hips to the right, so that his right hind leg does not have to swing as far forward as his left.

Other signs of a stiff left side are: the horse can turn left in a curve, but turns right by leaning his right shoulder inwards, keeping his body straight; at a canter he leads with his left front leg more easily than his right; when he walks or trots in a 'straight' line, his right hind foot goes to the right of his front foot.

If you are to maximize the horse's power, you will have to loosen and straighten him. One way to check on his straightness and to supple

him is to trot in 6 metre circles (voltes).

The young horse above finds it hard to bend to the right. On the right, he is trying to keep his body straight and go round the corner shoulder first. When the rider tries to pull his head into the curve by using more rein, the horse simply pulls his head against the pressure.

Instead of putting a constant pressure on the inside rein, then, the rider (above left) plays with it with little squeezes. Gently but insistently, she coaxes the horse into giving to the rein rather than resisting it. But the trouble in fact is in the horse's back legs, not his head, and it is the rider's legs and back that are helping most. She has increased the pressure of her left leg behind the girth, her right leg at the girth, and is using her back, with more pressure on her inside seat bone, to drive the horse on.

The rider has also raised her left hand to help the horse bend his neck downwards and towards the inside rein. You can see, then, that although it seems natural to use more right rein when you are having trouble turning right, it is actually increasing the other aids and using less

The horse on the far left is bending his body in a smooth curve, but in the centre he is not: he is keeping his body straight and leaning his shoulder inwards. His left side is stiff, and he finds it hard to bend to the right.

On the right, you can see how a horse's spine bends. He cannot bend it more than this. When he turns a corner, or circles, his neck should be a smooth continuation of this curve. Here his neck is bent more than that, giving a kink where it joins his body.

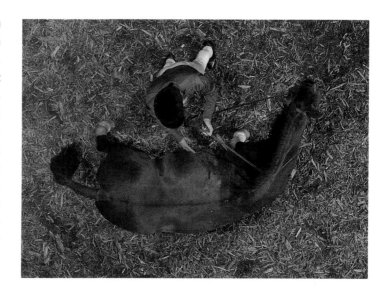

rein that produces the bend you want.

If you realize your horse is not moving straight, do check on your own straightness before assuming the horse is one-sided. A surprising number of people ride lop-sided, often with one stirrup lower than the other. The left leather stretches, because you use it for mounting, so it is no use checking that the holes match on both sides: take the stirrups off and measure them against each other. Make sure, too, that you are not always rising on the same diagonal when trotting.

You may also keep one rein tighter than the other, particularly if you have been taught to take a 'contact'. Most beginners are far too tense to realize how hard they are gripping, and put a heavier weight on their stronger side (usually the right). The horse's mouth is then deadened on that side, and he leans on that rein, so making you more lop-sided. Usually you do not notice until you ride a more sensitive horse.

At the volte you will of course use a sitting trot so you can use your back well. You can do a volte or two in each corner of your school as

you go round; or you can start by making a big circle, gradually make it smaller, then open it out again. Keep the rhythm of your trot active and even. It is a great help to find a song that matches the rhythm of your horse's working trot, and sing it throughout, in other exercises as well. You notice far better when the horse slows down because he is finding the work difficult, or if his paces are uneven. If he does not reach his back feet equally far forward, his steps will be uneven. The more effort he makes, the more uneven his rhythm.

Straightening and suppling the horse will take several weeks of work: if you attack the problem too vigorously, you will make the horse stiffer at first, which he will resent. Try to use opportunities out hacking to practise the odd volte. If you do a volte round a tree, you will notice far better whether he is doing the same going right or left.

When a horse does perfect voltes, his back feet follow exactly in the tracks of his front feet. You can ask a friend to check this. The horse above left has swung his hindquarters out.

Lunging

Make your circles large, 20 metres or so across. Drive the horse past you; do not try to lead him.

Lunging supples a horse and encourages him to use his back and back legs well.

Lunging is used for three main reasons: to exercise the horse when he is too young, weak in the back or silly to be ridden; to control him while a rider practises his position without reins; to educate the horse. Lunging well is a real art, much more difficult than it looks. If you are a novice at it, do not aim your sights too high at first, or you may do more harm than good. You need patience, good timing, praise and reward, and above all a critical eye for the horse's movement.

Since most horses turn left more easily than right, an inexperienced horse is taught to go left first, so he may get the idea without being in physical difficulty too. The work is hard in the beginning, so a few minutes is enough.

The horse wears a lunging cavesson, with the lunge line attached to the front ring. Over it he has a snaffle bridle, with side reins going to the surcingle. If you have no surcingle, you can attach them to the front girth pull. The side reins must have an elastic section in them so that there is never a hard feel on the horse's mouth: you can make this from a loop of strong elastic if necessary. They are fixed low on the

The lunger stands still and drives the horse in circles round her. She faces his middle, using the whip behind him to drive him, or pointing it at his shoulder to stop him coming towards her. On the left, the horse is moving well, pushing himself forward with his back raised and head stretched. This strengthens his loins and back legs. Above, he is moving badly, head raised, back dipped, and back legs out behind him.

surcingle and should not be tight: he should feel the rein only when he stretches down and forward. He should wear brushing boots lest he bang one foot on the other ankle.

If he does not recognize word commands, tell him what pace he is doing, rather than expecting him to know. Make your words sound as different as possible: 'walk on' rather than 'walk' (which sounds like 'whoa'); 'trrrott'; 'whoa' should be a long, calm sound. If you drop your whip and stand still, even slumping, the horse is likely to stop merely to see what has overcome you. Drop the rein and walk towards him to reward him before he comes to you.

Once the horse has grasped the idea well, concentrate on his movement. He should move briskly, with long, relaxed strides; his hind legs should reach well forward; his back should be raised; his neck will stretch forward and down until he reaches the limit of the side reins. Whenever he does this well, praise him warmly as he goes, then stop him so that he understands what it is you approve of.

If he has difficulty on the right rein (clockwise), do not expect too much at first. Walking well in large circles with the right amount of curve (i.e. with his back feet following his front feet) will do him more good than trotting in smaller circles with his body set wrong because he is uncomfortable. You can supple yourself by pushing yourself until it hurts, because you know it will do you good in the end. You cannot ask the same of a horse. He has no aim except to be comfortable, and if you force him into an uncomfortable position he will become tense and miserable, and the tension may damage his back. So take your time. Ask him to do easy things perfectly, and increase your demands only very gently. You will see him try out all sorts of different ways of moving, especially at first. Look for free, relaxed, happy-looking movement that goes with a good rhythm and swing, and praise him for it.

Lunging is an excellent way of teaching a slow, relaxed canter, but again this is fraught with difficulty. Do not ask for it until he trots well on both reins, and is calm and relaxed. He is liable to rush off at first, trying to turn Western-style, with his body leaning in and his head turned out. If the lunge rein pulls his head in, he may slip. If he keeps trying to strike off (lead) on the outside leg, draw his head in gently with the lunge rein as you urge him on.

Working him over poles is a good way of asking him to lower his head and raise his back if he does not seem to hit on the idea himself.

When you are sure he is using his hindquarters well (which will take weeks), you can shorten the side reins slightly. The brief, elasticated tugs on the rein mimic the squeezing action of your hands, asking him to begin to rebalance himself. If you do this too early he will go above or behind the bit, so go carefully.

Straightening the horse: the shoulder-in

General de l'Hotte, Chief Instructor at the French Cavalry School, Saumur, wrote, 'calm, forward, straight'. If the horse is not calm, he is unresponsive. If he does not move forward well, he develops no power. If he is not straight, he develops power unevenly. What is not clear is that you straighten a horse by bending him, making supple the stiff side until he does walk straight when you want him to.

The shoulder-in is one of a family of exercises in which the horse is asked to move forward with his body bent, so that his hind feet do not follow his front feet. It supples and straightens the horse, but he must be reasonably well balanced to do it.

The horse on these pages is moving down the long side of the school in a straight line. However, his body is bent in a smooth curve, as if he were making a small circle to the left, with his shoulder turned in to the inside of the school. He drops his rump as he reaches forward and under himself with his inside hind leg.

As with all more advanced work, you will get the feeling much better if you first try it on a trained horse. Bend the horse round a corner of the school, then continue straight on with his body bent in the same curve. You will have to increase the pressure of your inside leg on the girth in order to keep him going forward, and

the pressure of your outside leg behind the girth to keep his hindquarters from hitting the side of the school. Keep your weight slightly on your inside seat bone; take care that you are not slithering to the outside or you will hamper the horse.

Watch for the smooth bend of his body. When he is bent like this, his legs cross as the inside ones reach in front of the outside ones. It is the way his inside back leg reaches forward and towards the middle of his girth that stretches and increases the suppleness of his opposite side. You will also have to use your outside, indirect rein to push the horse's shoulders inwards.

A stiff horse, or one that has never been asked for a shoulder-in, will try to avoid bending by turning his head to one side while moving straight forward. This, of course, defeats the point of the exercise. The bend of his neck should continue in a smooth curve all the way down his spine. He may, especially if he is older and more fixed in his ways, think you mean him to turn inwards in a circle. It is your inside leg driving him forward that shows him this is not what you want. But if he is extremely resistant to the idea, try asking for a shoulder-in down a narrow lane, where he cannot turn without hitting the opposite side. Praise him the moment he seems to understand

what you mean, and let him relax before you try again.

When the horse is stiff, you will not be able to ask for much bend, or you will get a kink where his neck joins his body. You will also find it easier one side (probably the left) than the other. Work the good side before the bad;

the bad will improve. When you can, do it in a slow, collected trot.

On a reasonably supple horse you will find he is moving on three tracks. His inside front footprints go in a straight line. His inside hind foot follows his outside front foot in another line, nearer the outside of the school. His outside back foot makes another line. You will not achieve this degree of bend at first, but you must work towards it, aiming for perfection at easier angles. This horse is so supple that he is moving at an even sharper angle. Since the point of doing a shoulder-in is to make the horse supple, there is no particular angle that is 'correct': you ask for as much bend as the horse can do without losing his smooth curve.

The horse cannot do this well unless his balance is shifted to the rear, so you may need to do a half-halt before starting a shoulder-in. When you have done a few steps, move him inwards on a circle, using the same bend, but do not let him drop his balance.

Suppleness and power: the half-pass

It is unlikely that you will perfect the next few exercises without a good teacher and experience on trained horses. They need, and test, a high degree of suppleness and power. Many people are put off trying them because so much emphasis is put on the standards required for dressage competitions. It is true that, if that is your aim, it is a mistake to try them without expert guidance, lest your horse develop sloppy habits, But if you simply want to make your horse lighter, more manoeuvrable and more fun to ride, go ahead. If you do not get them quite right, you will not develop your horse's athletic ability to the maximum, but you will do him no actual harm. Aim for perfection at slow paces in the beginning.

At a half-pass the horse moves half-forward, half-sideways, by crossing his legs under him. His body is slightly bent in the direction he is going, that is, 45° to the angle of his body. The rider is using his right leg strongly behind the girth to push the horse's hindquarters sideways; his left leg pushes at the girth to keep him going forward; he has a very slight open rein, and is using his indirect rein to move the horse's shoulder sideways. He puts his weight on his right seat bone to help the sideways movement. Most of all he uses his back to encourage the horse to coil his back under him and reach forward with his back legs.

A perfect half-pass is a joy to ride or to watch: the horse feels as if he were floating lightly. The rhythm of his collected trot is kept so that, like a waltzer, he sweeps forward or sideways with hypnotic grace.

On a trained horse, first make sure the horse is going forward in good balance. Come round the corner of the school, keep a slight flexion in the same direction and, facing the end of the school, shift him diagonally across it to the

opposite corner. Unless you keep your back and legs active, he will run out of power. You will find it easier to push him sideways if you time your outside leg push to arrive as he is about to put his outside leg down.

This is of course the same use of your leg that you saw earlier (page 62), but there you were not asking the horse to bend in the direction he was going. On your own horse, then, start from this use of the leg. If he does not respond well, practise your turn on the forehand to sharpen up his response (do remember the praise). When you can push him

sideways as he walks forward on a loose rein, ask him to rebalance himself by using your back and inside leg well. Use your indirect rein on his shoulder. Do not worry about the 45° angle at first. Concentrate instead on keeping his body going straight forward, with just the smallest suggestion of a bend in the direction you are going. His back legs should not lag behind his front ones. If they do, you are using too much rein and not enough outside leg.

45° is the angle of the true half-pass, the standard exercise; but a horse can of course move part-sideways at any angle he wants. There is no reason why you should not do quarter-passes, or one-third-passes, or whatever. They are a wonderfully neat and elegant way of moving sideways to avoid traffic.

Once your horse recognizes what you are asking for at the walk, he will naturally want to rebalance himself to do it at the trot. He will then feel beautifully light.

The full pass

Classically, the advanced movements are taught from the ground ('in hand'). The trainer uses his whip instead of his leg to move the horse sideways. This is highly skilled work.

In the full pass or side step the horse moves completely sideways. He keeps his body straight or slightly bent in the direction he is going. He moves each diagonal pair of legs together: thus when he is moving to the left, his left front leg steps wide while his right back leg steps under his body, crossing in front of his left back leg. In the next step, his right front leg crosses in front of its partner, while his left back leg steps wide.

This movement forms part of the education of the classical horse since it is an extremely handy move in battle or bullfighting; as it is also useful when you have approached the wrong end of a gate, and in many tight spots, most Western horses are taught it. However, it is no longer required in modern dressage competitions.

The horse must be well balanced, or he cannot move his front end sideways; he must be powerful behind, or he cannot move his hindquarters sideways with his weight on them; and he must be supple, or he cannot reach his back foot across under his body. If he lacks the balance and power, he will merely shuffle uncomfortably sideways, not crossing his feet.

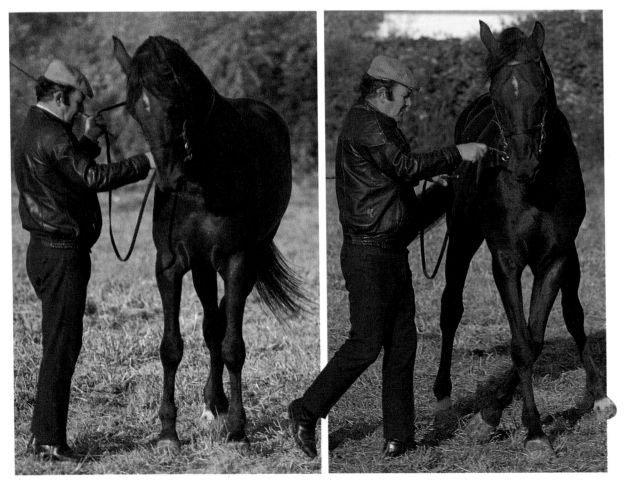

In the classical tradition the full pass is developed from a half-pass by gradually increasing the angle and decreasing the amount of forward movement.

Westerners follow the traditional maxim: make it easy for the horse to do the right thing, and difficult or impossible to do the wrong one. Put a big solid pole half a horse's length away from, and parallel to, a fence. Raise it to the height of the horse's knees. Step his front legs over it, facing the fence. Use your outside leg and outside rein to ask him to move sideways, helping his balance and power with your weight and back. Even if the horse does not understand what he is being asked, there is little he can do except move sideways: he cannot step forward, and he finds it almost impossible to step backwards over the bar.

This method is easier for a Western-trained horse to understand than a English-trained one, for he more readily moves his front end away from a neck rein, and he knows how to use his back-end power. But any willing and sensitive horse that is calm about solving problems will see, with your help, that there is only one solution to his predicament and move correctly.

With a difficult movement such as this you must remember that you cannot expect much at first. You must be patient and keep the horse calm. Reward and praise him the moment he even suggests moving sideways, then let him relax. When you ask again, he will be encouraged to try more. An older horse may well think it a very odd request. Having a friend help push him sideways may make the point clearer. Once he understands, he will improve with practice; but if you are disappointed with the results, remember that the key lies in the horse's balance, suppleness and power.

Teaching your horse the full pass is a good test of how well you understand the importance of patience, calmness, reward and good timing, as well as his responsiveness.

The full pass used to be called 'passage' in England, which is confusing since the French *passage* means a highly elevated slow trot (page 48).

The rider uses his right leg behind the girth to push the horse sideways, and his left leg on the girth to maintain power and keep the horse slightly bent in the direction he is going.

The flying leg change

When a cantering horse wants to change the leg he is leading on, he usually does so in mid-air. For instance, if he is on his left lead, his stride actually begins with his right back leg. If he wants to change to the right lead, he switches the angle of his body when all his legs are in the air, starting the next stride with his left back leg. This is called a 'flying change'. Almost certainly you will have felt this happen while out hacking, when the horse changed direction.

The rider here has asked for a flying change on a straight line. This is much more difficult, for the horse must be so well balanced that he is highly sensitive to the aids.

As you can see, he changes legs behind first. During the stride before the change, the rider has shifted her aids from left to right, sliding her left leg back and right leg forward. As the horse rolls forward on to his left front leg, she pushes with her left leg to shift his hindquarters

to the right, so helping him to put his left back leg down first. During her left-lead canter, her left hip is naturally slightly in front of her right (try to feel that while cantering). As the horse is in mid-air, she switches to having her right hip leading.

All this is done so subtly as to be barely noticeable. In fact, on a very well-balanced horse all you really need to do is to twitch your hips to ask him to change leads.

This sounds dreadfully complicated. Put more simply, she changed the horse's bend, making it slightly uncomfortable for him to keep cantering on the right lead; then she helped him along in the change as he was flying. It feels as if you warn the horse, then pick him up with your back as he is flying and put him down on the other lead.

One of the most difficult dressage exercises, and most delightful to watch or ride, is the

flying change at every stride. But it is not so difficult, if your horse is well balanced and supple, to teach him to do a flying change at the cross-over point of a figure-of-eight. If your figure-of-eight is fairly small, your turning aids will be quite pronounced, so the shift from one direction to the other will be more obvious.

As you come up to the cross-over, change the horse's bend, then push with your seat bone on the side you are changing towards. Clearly, your horse must be happy to canter on either lead. If he is not, he is stiff on one side, and you will have to work at loosening it.

You can also do it in counter-canter, as shown here. Make a figure-of-eight, but deliberately do not change legs. Instead, go into the next corner leading on the outside leg; then make the change.

The commonest fault is for the horse to change legs in front before he changes behind.

That is, he switches his front lead at the end of one stride, goes disunited (see page 37) for one stride, then changes behind at the beginning of the next stride. This does not feel at all delightful: it feels jerky, lumpy and unbalanced. In a true flying change you feel as if you were floating. Unless the horse is moving extremely slowly, only a skilled observer will see the fault, so you must rely on your feeling. It means that the horse is not really supple and well balanced; go back to doing exercises to help the horse, rather than trying to force him to do flying changes before he is physically able, or he may wrench the muscles in his back.

The flying change is difficult, and the horse may get over-excited. Do not overdo it, and do remember the praise. Once you have mastered it, you will find it extremely useful in fast games such as polo, horseball or gymkhana.

At the far left, the horse is in counter-canter, that is, leading on his outside (left) leg. His body is slightly bent to the left. When the rider subtly reverses the bend, he reverses the order of his back legs as they come forward, then flips his front legs in the air to reverse them. He continues on his right lead. The change from right to left lead is usually easier at first.

The pirouette

Classical training or dressage takes movements that are useful in a working horse, like the half-pass and flying change, and raises them to an art form. Great attention is paid to slow, even rhythms and absolute precision of control. The classical pirouette is one of the loveliest of these movements but requires a wonderfully balanced, supple and powerful horse to be done perfectly. But if you understand the idea, you should be able to do faster part-pirouettes on any handy horse, and you will find him far more manoeuvrable at a canter.

Pirouettes belong to the same family of turns as the turn on the haunches, roll-back (page 144) and spin (page 146). The horse drops his

bottom, puts his hind feet well forward under him and turns his front end round them. In a pirouette he keeps the slow, graceful rhythm of the collected canter. A full pirouette (360°) is done in six to eight strides, a half-pirouette in three or four.

The horse here is slightly bent in the direction he is turning. He is cantering properly, with a flying stage, throughout the turn, but his inside hind leg is merely going up and down on the same spot.

A perfect, full pirouette is extremely strenuous: the horse carries almost all his weight on his back legs for several seconds, turning the while. But if your horse is well balanced and active enough to canter a small half-volte without losing power, you can begin the work. Before you go into your volte, push the horse's hind legs well under him with your back; rebalance him with a half-halt; then make your half-volte by turning his forehand more than his hindquarters. His hindquarters will not stay in the same place, but they will make a smaller circle than his front legs. Bit by bit you can come closer to the true pirouette. You will find the horse catches on quicker if you do it in the same place at first, then change to other places.

If you are more interested in usefulness than style (as, for instance, in polo), you will find it helpful to use your weight a little more than is considered permissible in pure dressage; you may also find it helpful to put your outside leg forward, tapping your toe against his shoulder to move it over.

The main problem is to maintain the horse's power throughout the turn, or he will slow or stop. If he does, ride him straight forward immediately. Clearly, the slower and more complete the turn, the more difficult it is.

The educated horse

This horse is doing a *piaffe*, a high, beautiful trot on the spot. Only through patient, thoughtful training can he do this extremely difficult pace calmly and elegantly. See how he is carrying almost all his weight on his back legs, with his balance tipped to the rear.

In closing the gate, on the far right, horse and rider make a series of precise movements equally calmly and harmoniously.
They stop parallel to the gate.
They make a turn on the forehand, stepping back as the rider pulls the gate closed.
They turn away with a turn on the haunches, done one-handed.
They spring into a canter from a walk.

These are both educated horses, calm, well-balanced and responsive to the lightest touch. Yet their riders have very different aims. The classical rider perfects the formal school movements of that ancient tradition to display the highest equestrian art. His horse works almost entirely in the school. The boy wants a lively, manoeuvrable partner in games and adventures. He realizes that the precision and lightness he wants depend on the horse being 'calm, forward, straight' rather than on his recognizing the formal school movements. The horse has actually never been in a school; yet he is clearly an educated horse.

Any horse is as sensitive as these two, but few can respond so sensitively. A young, weak or badly balanced horse simply cannot move his body quickly in response. Any horse needs educating before he can carry himself and his rider in good balance. An older horse that has always been ridden badly will deliberately stiffen himself against the harsh aids that the rider finds he has to use, and so will appear more insensitive than he really is.

Whether or not you use a school to strengthen and educate your horse will depend on your aims and ability. But do be aware that school work does not necessarily educate a horse. Horses, like children, learn nothing from bad teaching except boredom, rebelliousness

The high school horse (below) must learn in a school to concentrate on difficult movements.

A more practical education makes this horse (right) equally responsive and knowledgeable.

and bad manners. What usually prevents a horse from improving is bad riding and bad teaching rather than wilfulness.

It is pointless, for instance, to ride carefully in the school and carelessly outside it. Your horse will merely learn to behave like you. It is pointless to trot endlessly around with a dead hand on the rein and the horse in bad balance. It is pointless, too, to become over-ambitious and concentrate too much on competition work, for the horse will lose his grace and brilliance.

It is also often pointless to school a young horse. The young horse cannot be asked to rebalance until he has enough power to hold himself up, and he only develops that power through free forward movement. In a school he usually feels inhibited and has to be driven, whereas outside his natural curiosity and *joie de vivre* draw him forward. It takes months of free movement on a loose rein before he develops enough strength for further work; and he will develop a happier attitude to being ridden, livelier paces, and a more alert intelligence if this work is done outside. By using natural situations imaginatively, you may well be able to complete his education without a school.

The school is invaluable when you are not sure of your control, when the horse is nervous, when you want him to concentrate on learning a new movement or, of course, when you want to excel in the formal school movements. But remember that those movements must not simply be drilled, rote-learned exercises, but full of brilliance, joy and life. Vary your work, both in the school and out, so that the horse is not bored, but takes a lively interest in learning.

'We shall take great care not to annoy the horse and spoil his friendly charm', said Pluvinel, 'for it is like the scent of a blossom – once lost it will never return.'

123

Using the power in jumping: approach and take-off

In jumping, especially over large fences, the horse must use his power suddenly and efficiently, coiling himself like a spring before he leaps. The changes in his balance and the shape of his body are fast and marked; he must calculate the timing precisely; and he must prepare himself for, and recover from, the effort. If he is nervous, his tension prevents him from using his body well: the good jumper is cool-headed and confident, as well as strong and fit.

As Caprilli saw, the rider's part in this is to hinder the horse as little as possible. This can only be done if you understand what his calculations involve. The experienced horse photographed here has been shown the jump and left to get on with it.

His approach is shown on the right (1., 2. and 3.). Although the jump is quite large, he is trotting slowly. His last stride before take-off is shown below (4.). He looks almost as if he were stopping. He stretches out his head, neck and front legs, extending his stride and lowering his body. In the next step he will reach his right front foot forward under his outstretched nose. From this position he can use his shoulder to lever himself forward and upwards (compare

1.

2.

3.

On the approach, the horse raises his head to be able to see the jump, and calculate its height and distance.

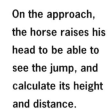

4.

124

7.

Above (7.), the moment of take-off, his spring continues smoothly. His head stretches forward and down; his back is round; his front legs fold and rise. His body is now at an angle of 40°.

In mid-air, centre top, his body is in a smooth upward curve, with his back raised and rounded, his neck arching forward and his head low. This curve is called the 'bascule'. A young or ignorant horse may not use his body in this way, but may fling himself over a jump with his head high and his back low. (Watch racehorses.) However, he will never be able to jump high like that. To make full use of his power he must coil his back and raise his loins, or he cannot bring his back legs far enough forward.

What you can see here is what you must allow your horse to do. He must raise his head to see the jump. He must extend his stride before take-off. He must use his shoulder in the first part of take-off, which he obviously cannot do if you are leaning forward on to it. He must raise his loins and round his back, which he cannot do with your weight on his back. He must tuck his nose in on take-off, and stretch his head and neck forward a split second later.

6.

the way he rises after rolling).

To the left (5.), he is coiling his back, bringing his back feet forward: notice the rise of the powerful muscles of his loins. To bring his back feet far enough forward for take-off, he must put them where his front feet are now. The lever action of his shoulder catapults his front end off the ground. His left front foot has already left the ground; his right front foot is about to rise as his left back foot touches down.

Above (6.), his back feet have landed, and his powerful hindquarters continue to thrust him upwards and forward. Again you can see how his back has coiled so his loins rise. He has tucked his nose in.

5.

Jumping: landing and recovery

His left foot now lands (below); he will be on his left lead in the next canter stride. As he lands, he raises his back and rump so his back feet can clear the jump. His head comes up, too; the curve of his back has suddenly reversed, like a whiplash. This clever horse twists his hips to avoid raising his rump more than absolutely necessary.

As he comes down (above), the horse stretches out his front legs, with one foot (here the right) in front. His back is not so rounded; his head and neck are stretched. The horse always lands on one foot; his pasterns must be strong to stand the impact of his whole weight travelling fast. He can change legs over the jump.

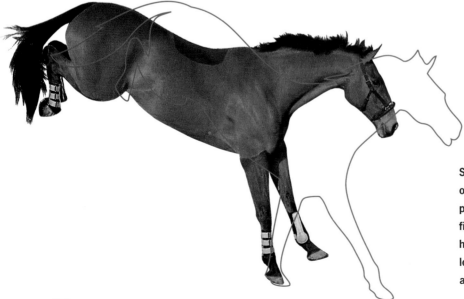

Superimposing the outline of the second photograph on the first shows how the horse's rump and loins rise suddenly as he lands.

Below, he rolls forward on to his front feet, pulling his back feet down after him so his loins rise again; then his downward, forward movement carries him over and past his front feet. Each back foot must land in front of the foot on the same side, which of course means that his front feet must move before his back ones can land. This is an extremely unbalanced position: he looks as if he were about to tip on to his nose, but for the fact that his right back foot has landed and can begin to support him and push him forward.

As his second back foot lands, his hindquarters can provide enough thrust and lift for him to reach forward with his front legs, but his balance is still well to the front. It will take a stride or two before he can recover.

In landing, then, you must stay well clear of his loins as he comes down. You must allow him to stretch his head forward for his first, extended stride; yet you cannot lean forward yourself, or your weight would tip him forward. He could not then save himself from rolling right over. If he stumbles at all on landing, you will both be in a difficult position, for you will have to help him hold himself up, though you will not be able to put your bottom in the saddle. You will have to rely on the deep heel and firm knee of the forward seat to help you.

Letting your horse jump free on a lunge rein will allow him to develop his style well, and will give you the chance to watch exactly what he does. Different horses develop slightly different techniques for getting their hind feet clear of the jump.

In the canter stride after landing he has not yet recovered his balance, which is still well forward. His stride is extended, as yours would be when hurtling downhill.

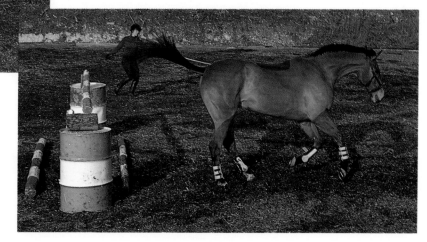

The forward seat in jumping

You must be firm yet supple in the saddle, with your weight in your heels and on your knees. You do not have to rise high: just support your weight so you are not hindering the horse's back movement (see page 52). Make sure you are not using the reins to help you balance. This rider's touch is light and sensitive.

To jump well you must
a) give the horse confidence
b) educate him both physically and mentally
c) interfere with him as little as possible.

Horses do not naturally volunteer to hurl themselves over large jumps, for their feet are at risk. However, most will come to enjoy jumping once they are confident. Much of this confidence depends on you: on your attitude, your teaching and your seat. No horse will jump if you hurt him by banging on his back or yanking at his mouth. He *cannot* jump if you upset his balance, or if your hands are too stiff to give to his natural head movements.

This is a larger jump than you will attempt at first, but it shows what you are aiming for. Note that the rider's weight is in her heel and that she never looks down (if you do, that is where you go).

On the approach she allows the horse to raise his head so he can see the jump properly. She is sitting upright, ready to push with her back if necessary.

On the last stride she allows him to extend. Notice she is not leaning forward. If she did, she would overload his front end, making it impossible for him to raise it as he gets his back

On this kind and well-educated horse the rider is deliberately leaving her reins slacker than usual, so that you can see that his head movements are his doing, not hers. Though her body folds and straightens, she never tips his balance forward. During the whole jump she keeps off his back.

feet forward under him. He would then stop; his body is perfectly positioned to do so.

As the horse uses his back powerfully to thrust himself upwards, the rider, too, rises. Her weight is a fraction ahead of his movement, which helps him. If she were more forward, she would prevent his rising; if she were left behind, she would stop his going forward. He needs to do both.

Over the jump she folds at the hip, letting her hands move forward with his head. Notice she has shifted her bottom back to balance the amount she has leaned her top half forward.

As they come down, she straightens but keeps her weight off his back in the critical moment of whiplash. Beginners often thump down on the horse here. It is particularly important not to, for his spine must first dip, then spring quickly up again as he draws his back feet forward. If she leaned forward here,

she would make it impossible for him to lift his front end before landing on his back feet.

She goes with him in his first, unbalanced stride. She will then sit more upright to help him regain a more even balance.

If you are lucky enough to ride a well-educated horse like this one, you can learn to feel the rhythm of a jump by working on a lunge or in a jumping lane (literally, a corridor with jumps built right across it) so that you do not need a bit in the horse's mouth. Almost all novice riders get left behind at first when the horse takes off, so they yank the reins and hurt the horse's mouth. Learn by holding a chunk of mane halfway up the horse's neck, or a neckstrap. Do not use a bit until you are certain you will not hurt the horse: in an enclosed space most horses are controllable in a headcollar, and will jump more willingly when they know they cannot be hurt.

Early work: banks and slopes

The changes in balance and angle that you have to cope with in jumping are dramatic, and very fast. Even over a small jump beginners get left behind, being thrown backward at take-off and (if they have survived that long) backward on landing. It is no fun for the horse, either.

The novice horse is not used to moving his body so athletically, and he tends to jump awkwardly.

depends on his control over his own balance: if he is unbalanced, or you unbalance him, he cannot respond easily. Keep your hands steady and he will steady himself. But let your feel on the reins be elastic, not rigid, and constantly try to lighten it so he has to find his own balance.

Cantering over bumps and dips helps him learn to change the length of his stride swiftly and easily, as he must when jumping.

If both of you are novices, then, you have problems. There is no way of slowing down a jump, but you can ride up and down banks and slopes to mimic these changes of angle and balance. Start slowly, only gradually increasing your speed. At first you will probably get left behind as he scrambles up, so hold his mane until you learn to rise as he does. It is usually the horse that has more of a problem going down. He tends to overbalance forward so that he rushes off. You will have to steady him with your hands until his control over his balance improves. He should be able to pop down a bank and walk away in balance.

Use dips, humps and slopes, and practise increasing your speed over those, too. Again you will find you are both a bit uncontrolled at first. Remember that your control over the horse

Jumping down small steps, even from a standstill, teaches you how to keep your weight off the horse's back when landing. Keep your weight in your heels, relaxing them so that they act as shock-absorbers as you hit the ground.

Once you can canter confidently over this kind of ground without either of you losing

A perfect place for learning to jump. You can do this at a walk at first, speeding up until you and your horse change your balance quickly and easily together.

Up and down steep slopes you learn to keep your weight off the horse's back and shift your balance with his.

your balance, you will almost certainly find that if you put a small jump across a well-known path both you and the horse will fly over it without any difficulty. He will have learned to use his back and his power well, and you will have learned to move with him.

This work is also excellent for the young horse or for the true competitor, who must not be overjumped. The young horse, if bold enough, may fling himself over a jump with his back dipped, not raised; but up steep slopes and banks he must raise his back in good style. Once he has learned to use his body well, he will naturally do so in jumping. The variety of the work helps to keep a horse keen as well as fit and handy. But you must use your imagination and wits, keeping an eye out for any opportunities.

Training the horse: trotting poles

Any horse can jump the height of his knees by doing what is basically a bouncy gallop stride. He takes the jump in the part of the stride after putting his back legs down and before his front legs hit the ground. A naive horse (and a naive rider) will think that the bigger the jump, the faster he must go. You can hurtle round the countryside quite merrily popping over small jumps in this way.

But there is a limit to this naive jumping. The horse cannot jump anything large. Over a large jump he needs a different technique: he must slow down, extend his stride and use his shoulder so that he can bring his back legs further forward under his body. Unlike other movements in this book, this is not one that horses practise when playing. They need to be taught. Expecting your horse to jump high, even if he jumps small jumps boldly and joyfully, is simply not fair unless he is well prepared: you will just shatter his nerve.

Look again at the horse on page 125. He took this large jump from a slow trot, using his power cleverly instead of relying on speed. Because of his education he is confident, calm and wise. This is beautiful jumping.

The first step in educating a jumper is trotting him over poles. This teaches him to measure his stride. He learns to extend himself with his back raised; he learns not to rush; and he learns about coloured poles and arena jumping. Any horse that gets over-excited or frightened about jumping will also be helped by going back to these basic lessons again.

Use long, solid poles. They must be evenly spaced at the length of his trot stride. For a horse this is just over a metre, or one long step of yours. A pony's stride is shorter, but his rider's step will be shorter, too. You can put your poles round part of a circle, so that they

are closer inside than outside, and find where the horse finds them easiest.

The horse's trot will be bouncy, and you want him to raise his back, so keep your weight off the saddle. Remember your aims: to keep a steady rhythm, neither speeding up nor slowing; to encourage the horse to stretch his neck and raise his back. If he does it in bad style, with his head raised and his back dipped, make the problem easier by using one pole, then two. In all basic training it is more important to do simple problems in good style than to do more difficult ones badly.

Once you are sure that you have got that right, you can ask for more. You can increase the spacing so he must extend his stride (but go gradually). You can raise the last pole to 30 centimetres; raise them all to 30 centimetres; double the distance of the last one and raise it to 50 centimetres; take out one in the middle, and so on. Keep the most difficult bits at the end of the set of poles. He will then learn to approach difficulties without rushing, for the earlier poles will slow him down.

A canter stride is about three times the length of a trot stride. If you now put two crossed poles as a low jump three long steps (your steps) beyond your last trot pole, the horse can trot or canter over it. Let him choose which he does. If you raise the last trot pole, he may be encouraged to canter it.

In this work you must get the distances between the poles right, or you will be asking the impossible. You must also leave his head free so he can stretch down to see. Remember to praise your horse when his style is good, or he will not know what you think is good.

You can also lunge your horse over poles. A young horse will think it a great game.

Trotting over poles makes this over-eager horse use his power instead of rushing. He strides out well, raising his back and reaching forward. His rider allows him to peer at the poles, then stays off his back.

Grids

Grids continue the work you began with trotting poles. A grid is a series of small fences carefully placed so as to develop the horse's athletic ability. These gymnastic exercises develop his body and his wits, so he learns to use himself cleverly. He cannot rush or take off in the wrong place, so he learns that jumping in good style, with his back raised and rounded, is comfortable and easy.

Before you start any jumping, warm the horse with gentle trotting and cantering. He cannot be athletic with cold muscles. You may want to repeat some trotting pole work.

Again you use the distances of the horse's strides to place your poles: one of your long steps for a trot, three for a canter. If you raise your poles to 50 centimetres, putting them three long steps apart, you should be able to canter neatly over them. Keep your rhythm steady. You can raise the last one to 70 or 80 centimetres, so it is more of a jump. You can take any of the middle poles out, so the horse does one flat stride before the next pole. You can replace any of the poles with a small jump. Or you can turn them all into small jumps, either with one flat stride between them or without. But you *must* keep the distances between them right.

One flat canter stride is about three of your long steps. Over a small jump he will cover a little more, say three and a half steps. If you want him to land and take off immediately over small jumps, then, put them three to three and a half steps apart. If you want him to take a stride, put them six to seven steps apart. Over a wide jump such as an oxer or a triple bar he will cover more ground than over an upright; you are best leaving these jumps to the last in a series.

The best jump for the start of a series, or for the start of your work wherever you put it, is a

pair of crossed poles. Any horse naturally jumps the middle of it, so at the start of the grid it sets him straight for the following jumps.

A single bar is difficult for a novice horse: he tends to take off too close and has to jump awkwardly. A ground pole in front of it will help him jump it comfortably. If it is the second of a pair put so that there is no stride between them (called a 'bounce'), your careful placing will make him take off in the right place.

It is a great help to have a friend watch you work. If your distances are not quite right, you will feel the horse jump awkwardly. It happens so fast that you probably will not be able to tell why, but your friend will.

Always aim for calmness and an even rhythm. If the horse rushes, go back to trotting pole work, then put your grid after the poles. If he runs out of steam, do more work on banks and slopes until he is fitter and more energetic; you can also use raised trotting poles to get him using his back legs more actively. He will jump more willingly facing towards his home.

If your horse rushes away after the last jump, help him to rebalance. A series of trotting poles several strides later will also slow him down.

At the end of a session when you have asked the horse to solve new problems, give him an earlier, easy one that he knows he can do. It keeps him cheerful.

This simple grid consists of three jumps. The crossed poles at the start encourage the horse to keep straight. The second, an upright, is three (rider's) steps away, so he lands and takes off immediately. The third, an oxer, is seven steps away, so he can land, take one canter stride, and take off again. The correct distances help the novice horse take the jump in good style. The 'bounce' between the first fences stops him rushing: a bounce always comes early in a grid. Note the rider's light touch and good balance.

Showjumping

Arena or show jumps should always be wide and solid-looking. When building courses at home, take care about the distances between them. You want the horse to jump with an unflustered, easy rhythm, so make it easy for him to get his strides right.

Gridwork makes the problems of jumping a course far smaller, for both you and the horse learn to judge distance and to rebalance quickly after each jump. The rider who practises only over a single jump tends not to understand the importance of balance in control, so that he cannot turn corners fast, or hurtles past a second jump. The half-halt technique is important here: use your legs and back to drive the horse's hind legs under him, your hand to check him and your weight to rebalance him (see page 105).

Over large jumps, the saying 'throw your heart over first and the rest will follow' is particularly true. Look at the space beyond the jump, willing yourself there, and both you and the horse will be far less daunted. Apart from education and confidence you must also consider your horse's conformation, his

physical shape, when tackling larger jumps. Only a horse with powerful back legs, and shoulders that allow him to extend himself, will ever jump high.

When competing, remember that high jumps put a terrific strain on a horse's legs and nerves. Once you know your horse can do them, save his ability for the important moments. Keep him agile on smaller jumps, or with imaginative hacking. Too many good horses have been ruined by over-practice or over-competing.

You may wonder why such stress has been put on approaching jumps slowly when so many competitors are 'against the clock'. Watch them and you will see the winners often seem to be moving slowly. They win by going less far, cutting the corners. Tight cornering depends on balance and technique, so work on those rather than speed itself.

If a horse starts refusing, start thinking and retraining immediately, before he stops jumping altogether. Remember your side of the partnership is intelligence, not anger; your patience, not your bullying.

This simple course is designed to be jumped in a circle or figure-of-eight either way. The rustic jump (right) is an oxer, or spread; the planks (left) are an upright; the combination has a stride between the jumps, so all need different techniques. Note the horse peering at the oxer; the way this experienced pair already turn as they land (right); how quickly they recover balance (left), so they can turn neatly, not wasting time.

Cross-country jumps

Cross-country jumps are usually lower, more natural-looking and further apart than show jumps, so the horse finds them easier; but they do not fall down when you hit them.

Even the casual cross-country jumper should check that the saddle fits the horse properly. In landing, the saddle jolts the horse's shoulders, so a badly fitting saddle puts the horse off. If you are not sure about yours, put a thick pad or blanket under it.

You can make good, unavoidable jumps across paths, gateways or gaps in hedges. They should look solid. Check the footing carefully. A horse can sprain himself if the ground is too soft or too hard; he can bruise his foot badly landing on a stone. He can also crack a bone

Above, a solid jump set into a hedge is inviting for the pony.

Left, in competition you will meet unusual jumps designed to unnerve you but not the horse. Use doors, beds, tables and your imagination at home, but keep free jumps wide.

Drop fences (right) are more frightening for the rider than the horse. Be sure to keep your weight off the horse's back when landing. Coming down banks is good practice for this.

Below, make piles of sticks lowest in the middle, and put them where the pony cannot run out. He will jump more willingly along a path he knows.

hitting a stone wall, so put a pole above it. Poles and short logs set upright can be used in many imaginative ways, while rows of straw bales make good puzzle jumps (check distances). A pole over a ditch is more inviting for the horse than an open ditch.

Many horses hate to jump water, so seize any opportunity to do it. Putting a pole on the take-off side is often helpful. Do not try to jump wire: at speed a horse cannot see it.

In competitions you must often keep to a certain speed, so check your time over a measured course at home. You must always walk a course first, checking the angle of attack and firmness of the ground. Check the landing especially, lest he stumble.

Using the power: Western-style

Western training was originally developed to produce a working cowpony, quick to turn, stop or accelerate to match the swift escape attempts of nippy young cattle. He must, therefore, bring his hind legs well forward under his body to make maximum use of his power. Unlike the classically trained horse, he must carry his head low so that his rider can rope a fleeing steer without hitting his ears. He must also use his intelligence, working out his footing on rough ground, understanding how to keep the rope tight while his rider attends to the cow, or noticing cattle hiding in underbrush. He is a true working partner.

This stock horse display mimics ranch work. As the rope snakes out over his head and touches the ground (or lassos the cow's legs), the horse stops. Notice his superb use of his back legs, which carry his weight as he throws his balance backward. He is not being hauled back – his rider is beginning to dismount – but has been trained to understand his work.

As the rider tugs on the rope, imitating the struggling steer, the horse backs away by himself to keep the rope tight. This teamwork, reliant on the horse's wisdom and co-operation, is a delight to watch. The Western horse's superb agility depends on his excellent balance and powerful hindquarters.

Once he has been trained to respond lightly to the aids in a bosal (page 152) or snaffle, he is taught on the curb (bit or hackamore) to use his body and balance well in turns and stops.

A good deal of emphasis is placed on backing, when the horse's head is low, his back raised, his hindquarters low and his hind legs well forward. Thus he is asked to reverse before turning on his haunches, or after stopping, even at slow paces. As his balance improves, the speed of the work is increased. On a fast-working horse the rider often has to hold the horn to steady himself against the horse's violent changes of direction and balance. Although the rider always has full control, his loose rein and supple seat allow the horse to use his body naturally, and often to make his own decisions.

Competition work includes rodeo sports such as calf-roping, team-roping (two riders roping head and heels of a calf) and barrel-racing; cutting, where the horse literally dances head to head with a calf; equitation classes such as Western pleasure or trail riding (slow work through difficult obstacles); stock horse classes, which test working skills; and reining classes, the high-speed dressage of the Western world.

Western-style riding, with its loose rein and use of the horse's intelligence, often suits Arabs, although strictly speaking their natural head carriage is too high for ranch work. Any Western-trained horse can equally well be ridden European-style: the different tack naturally produces a different carriage, and the horse is light to any aids. A Western horse will never lean on the bit.

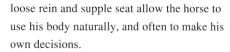

Fast stops

A Western horse must be able to stop immediately from a flat-out gallop. He plants his back feet firmly under his body and sits back on them. If he does this on dry, dusty ground, he will produce the famous sliding stop seen in reining contests.

The ideal stop is square, straight and final. The horse does not bounce, overbalance forward or slew to one side: he sits down. If you look again at the loose horse stopping suddenly (page 72), you can see that this is the natural way.

Nevertheless, the horse must be carefully trained to reach this stage of performance, for it is essential to stop on a loose rein. If you suddenly yank on the reins, the horse throws his head up. When he does this, his back dips and he is unable to get his back legs forward under himself. He cannot stop immediately, for he cannot sit down. It is only when his head is free that he can use his body naturally in these dramatic stops and turns; and his head is only free when there is no direct pressure on the bit.

The horse is therefore trained from the earliest stage to respond to the rider's weight and the voice command 'ho!' These aids are given *before* the rein is used. Little by little he realizes that by responding to them quickly enough he avoids having pressure put on his mouth or nose. When he is ridden in a curb, which is far more powerful than a snaffle or bosal, his eagerness to avoid rein pressure sharpens his response still further.

Teaching the horse to respond quickly to weight, neck rein or voice in order to avoid the curb is the basis of a great deal of Western riding. It depends on careful training. Your timing of the aids must be precise, the rein always being used last; the idea must be well established in calm, slow work before any faster work is tried; reward and praise will speed the learning.

When considering fast stops, look at the ground carefully. Since the horse's back feet are well forward, his fetlocks may hit the ground, so avoid hard or stony places; fetlock boots are a good idea. But do not try fast stops until the horse can handle sudden stops from walk or trot confidently, or you will hurt him and produce tension and resistance.

Since the horse stops with low hindquarters, it is easier for you to dismount before he has recovered his balance. If you do not dismount, back him up a couple of paces, especially if you are aiming at roping work. He will then start to take some of the strain on the rope before you have run to your calf. However, if you back him up every time, he will assume that it is part of the stop, so vary your demands.

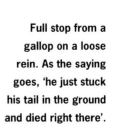

Full stop from a gallop on a loose rein. As the saying goes, 'he just stuck his tail in the ground and died right there'.

The roll-back

In a 'roll-back over the hocks' the horse gallops, makes a fast 180° turn on the haunches ('over the hocks') and gallops away on the same track as he arrived on.

The horse shown here comes into a clockwise roll-back on his right lead. He stops with his rump lowered. He throws his weight back on to his hocks and pivots to the right: he is carrying his weight on his back legs and using his front legs to push himself round fast. He gallops back along his previous track, thrusting himself powerfully forward, still on his right lead.

In practice the roll-back is so fast that you cannot see, as you can here, the three separate

elements that make it up: a stop, followed by a pivot, and finally a quarter-pirouette at a gallop. Notice the difference between this and the fast turn (page 82): there the horse galloped in a tight circle, while here he turns on the spot, on his back legs. The true roll-back of 180° is the one asked for in any performance test, but this type of turn, of different degrees, is often used in ranch work, for the horse changes direction faster than when galloping in a circle. If you

look again at the pictures on page 79 (lower right) or page 96, you will see that it is what a horse naturally does when he wants to make a sharp turn at speed.

Again you want to avoid interfering with the horse's head position, so before you start work on the roll-back make sure you can stop on a loose rein, with the horse's back legs forward under him. Only when his hind legs are forward can he swing his front end round. Practise first at a walk, but hurry him out of the turn. If he does not make the pivot move well, ask him to back before pivoting, for this will place his hind legs better. He does not actually have to step backward, merely to rock his weight back on to his hind legs.

You may find it easier to walk the horse alongside a fence and make your roll-back inwards from the fence. The horse will tuck his bottom down better, fearing to hit the fence. Use your weight backward as well as sideways to help him throw his weight back during the pivot; then urge him forward and sideways in the next pace, using your outside leg behind the girth to stop his hindquarters drifting out. Experiment with the balance of your aids until you can make the moves slickly.

You cannot perfect a true roll-back by simply trying to turn sharply at a gallop. Aim for perfection at a slow pace before trying to speed up. The horse must stop with his back legs together if he is to make a good pivot; he must push with his outside foreleg and step on to his inside one; and his head must be low, or he cannot step wide. He cannot be expected to do these moves at a lope or gallop unless he understands them well at a walk.

At a lope watch your leads. The horse must turn towards his leading leg, for his balance is already rolling that way.

The spin

Each stride is a pivot, the outer foreleg pushing the horse's front end over while his hind legs carry his weight: look at the powerful muscles in his hindquarter.

A spin is a complete 360° turn on the spot, done as fast as possible. The approach and exit are made at a gallop.

This is one of the most spectacular moves that a ridden horse is ever asked to make. It has no everyday use, being a demonstration of a horse's use of his power and manoeuvrability on a loose rein.

In a good spin the horse's head is low so that he can spread his forelegs wide: a series of forced rearing hops is not a spin. His inside back foot stays in the same place, swivelling round on what is normally soft, dusty ground. In these respects it differs from a high-speed version of a pirouette, where the action is higher in front and the horse's hind feet must

lift and fall in the canter rhythm.

You develop a spin from a 360° series of pivots. Only a truly well-balanced horse, with strong hocks, will be able to spin fast and easily. Asking the horse to spin faster than he is physically able will only hurt him and provoke his resentment. Even a horse that can spin well will resent overdoing it. In all forms of higher training, patience is the trainer's best aid.

Begin your spin work slowly, encouraging the horse to bring his hind legs right forward so that they can hold his weight. As his speed increases, take care about the ground you are working on. His back foot should slide round as he swivels on it; if it sinks down, he will strain his pasterns.

The action is so fast you can barely see what is happening. The horse's head and rump are low; he has rocked his weight back on to his back legs.

The bridle: snaffle bits

What you put in your horse's mouth greatly affects his way of going. If he is afraid of his bit, he will never move freely and confidently, and may develop a number of horrible habits to escape his fear and pain. On the whole, the gentler your bit and hands, the less the horse wants to fight you.

In theory, one bit affects all horses in the same way. In practice it does not, for horses' mouths vary greatly in shape and sensitivity. If your horse seems unhappy with his bit, even when you are sure you use your hands gently and sensitively, experiment with different bits.

There are scores of different bits, but they fall into two main types: snaffle and curb. The fatter and lighter the bit, the more comfortable.

Tightening the rein presses the bit against the bars and tongue. The horse relaxes his jaw and brings his nose closer to his chest by bending at the very top of his neck (poll). Stand beside your horse to make sure he does this.

Snaffle bits

These act on the horse's mouth. The bit lies over the horse's tongue, in the gap between his front and back teeth, on the gums, or 'bars'. This type should fit snugly into the corners of the mouth; a jointed snaffle is hung slightly higher. If it is too low, it will act suddenly and harshly; the horse may also put his tongue over it. If it is too high or narrow, it will bruise his lips, while too wide a bit will rub the corners of the mouth.

When you put a bridle on, open the horse's mouth by putting your thumb in the corner, where there are no teeth. If you merely force the bit against his teeth, you will hurt him.

This fat rubber bar is the gentlest type of bit, especially suitable for a young or tender-mouthed horse. It is slightly curved to allow for the bulge of the horse's tongue. Beware of very soft ones: they bend so much that they rub the corners of the mouth. If the horse chews through the rubber, use a curved vulcanite (hard plastic) bar. It does not bend but is gentle, light and comfortable.

A jointed snaffle has a far harsher action: if you put much pressure on it, it squeezes the sides of the horse's jaw like a nutcracker, while the joint may hit the roof of the mouth. This is a German hollowmouth eggbutt: hollow so it can be fat where it touches the bars without being heavy; eggbutt because of the way the rings are fixed. This is the kindest of the jointed snaffles.

A loose-ring jointed snaffle is usually used in racing. The rings can pinch the corners of the mouth, so rubber rings are used for protection.

When a horse is hurt by the pressure of the snaffle, or wants to ignore it, he stiffens his neck and sticks his nose up and out. The pressure is taken off the bars, so he will not stop. If you ride with your hands high, you change the angle of the reins so the same thing happens.

You will notice that showjumpers, whose horses are fit and keen, usually carry their hands extra-low to prevent this happening. They also use running martingales, straps which run from the horse's girth to rings round the reins. When the horse raises his head, as he must when approaching a high jump, the martingale makes the rein and bit act at the right angle.

In ordinary riding you should not need a martingale. Most people who use them do so because their hands are so rough that their horses are constantly trying to avoid painful pressure. Improve your hands rather than forcing the horse to suffer pain.

A horse may also stick his lower jaw to one side so he clamps the bit and stops it acting as a nutcracker; or he may open his mouth wide to take the pressure off the roof. Such a horse often finds his jaw strapped tight with a noseband. Although he can be stopped, the bit still hurts him, and he cannot relax his jaw and accept it. But a horse that constantly fights the bit should (a) have his mouth examined in case he has teeth in odd places (b) be tried in different bits (c) be re-educated, gently and patiently, with thoughtful work in a school, until he accepts the bit of his own free will. You will get better results if you first stand in front of him and play gently with the reins, encouraging him to relax and bend at the poll. Holding a reward behind his chin will help.

Curb bits

A curb bit has straight side pieces (shanks) and an unjointed mouthpiece. It acts on the horse's chin and poll more than on his mouth. A chain or strap runs between the shanks round the back of the horse's jaw, above his soft chin. The shanks act as a lever, tightening the chain. Because of this lever action, curbs are less avoidable than snaffles, and horses tend to respect them more. This means that they must

always be used by careful riders with good hands. A horse that is harshly ridden in a snaffle can learn to escape the pain by stiffening his jaw; in a curb he cannot, and he may resort to rearing or running backward.

Like snaffles, curbs vary in severity. The longer the shank, the harsher the action. The tighter the chain, the quicker it acts. The chain may be padded for gentler action.

Curb action. When the rein tightens, the shanks tilt. The top part goes forward so the bridle tightens over the poll, lowering the horse's head. The lower part pulls back so the curb (the chain) tightens; the horse bends at the poll to tuck his nose in. The chain is twisted so that the links lie flat before being fastened, and is adjusted so that it acts when the shanks are at an angle of 45°.

The Pelham has two reins. The upper one acts on the bit (here rubber-covered), giving the gentle action of a curved bar; the lower one acts on the curb and poll. Although the snaffle and curb actions are not as separate as in a double bridle (right), this can be a handy everyday bit, for the mouthpiece itself is mild.

Some horses, like this one, do not like the nutcracker action of the jointed snaffle, perhaps because their bars are tender or the roof of the mouth is low so the joint hits it. Such a horse is best ridden in a rubber bar. But an excitable and energetic horse (this one is a stallion, so he sometimes has strong feelings in mixed company) can raise his head, avoid the action of

the bit and leap forward uncontrollably. In this Pelham he can be ridden on the snaffle rein for most of the time; the curb rein is only used to bring his head down when he resists the snaffle action. This means, of course, that the rider must be able to operate the two reins independently, which takes practice.

The Pelham can also be used as a corrective for a horse that has learned to lean on a snaffle, or will not bend at the poll. Again the snaffle rein is used first; the curb is played gently only if the horse resists.

It must be stressed that using a curb bit will only lead to far worse problems if your hands are harsh and heavy.

Curb bit (Weymouth) for a double bridle. The raised 'port' in the middle takes pressure off the tongue. There is only one rein.

Western grazing bit. A softer strap replaces the chain, and the shanks are swept back so the horse can graze. There is only one rein, but it is seldom used directly; the reins are always loose.

A double bridle (above) has two bits, a light snaffle and a curb, so that the horse's head can be raised or lowered precisely. This is the bridle used in dressage. In good hands, any horse carries himself better in a double bridle; in bad hands, he panics, for the snaffle (called a 'bridoon') is of necessity thin.

The bridoon is hung above the curb. The reins are held separately, as shown. One rein goes between the third and fourth fingers; the other runs between the fourth and little fingers. When extra action of the lower rein is needed, it can be played with the little finger above it. Practise this action with somebody holding the bit before trying it on a horse.

Some people ride with the curb rein on top, as shown here. The curb rein is slack or almost so, merely reminding the horse to bend at the poll. The snaffle rein is played when an open rein is needed. Others use the snaffle rein on top, playing the curb rein only when needed. This is more usual when using the curb as a corrective for retraining. Yet others, notably in the Spanish Riding School, ride with both curb reins (and one snaffle rein) in one hand.

Bitless bridles

Bitless bridles are traditionally used in Arab, Spanish and Western riding. Again they vary in severity, from extremely gentle to really brutal (not shown here). Horses with damaged mouths, tender or odd-shaped mouths, or teething problems especially welcome a bitless bridle. So do many Arab horses, whose large tongues, narrow jaws and extreme sensitivity can make bitting a problem.

When a horse is afraid, he tightens his mouth, tips his head up and stiffens his neck. In this position he does not respond easily. If he is afraid of your hurting his mouth, removing the bit removes his tension, often changing his behaviour remarkably. The curb of the hackamore tends to lower his head and encourage him to bend at the poll, thus improving his carriage still further. Note that it is harsh handling of a bit that causes the problem in the first place: a horse that has always been calmly ridden with light hands accepts his bit happily.

A bosal or hackamore must not hang too low on the nose or it can damage the small, delicate bones there. You cannot ride with a constant pressure on a hackamore, and the open rein has little effect: you have to use your balance, legs, and indirect or neck rein more. This actually improves your riding, making you less reliant on your hands; but a horse that has been sloppily ridden in a snaffle will need retraining.

You can improvise a bitless bridle by riding on a headcollar or attaching the reins to the rings of a drop noseband, hung high and padded (see page 68). If you find you need a curb action to stop, slip a strap round the back and through the rings, and attach the reins to the ends of it. This is a kind way to start riding a young horse, or to allow a child or beginner to ride a sensitive horse.

A bosal (above) is a rawhide loop. It is especially used in training the Western horse, but a gentle, sensitive horse will be fully controllable in it all his life. The angle it hangs at is adjusted by the cord throat latch and by the weight of the knot at the back. Both reins attach there, so there is no open-rein action.

The Western hackamore (left) has a curb, so the action is now on nose and curb, bringing the horse's head in. The top of the shank swivels, so the action is only on the curb at first. If the horse pulls strongly, his nose and poll are increasingly affected.

A well-trained hackamore horse is delightfully light to ride, for he can be asked to rebalance himself well. He is instantly manoeuvrable and capable of all the advanced dressage movements on a completely loose rein. However, you may not enter dressage competitions without a bit. This is because of tradition rather than ability.

The European hackamore (below) is far more severe. The plate tilts so that the bridle tightens over the poll, the noseband clamps down on the nose and the curb acts. Even a large and powerful horse can be stopped in this.

Nosebands and other gadgets

When a horse accepts the bit, he relaxes his jaw, sometimes so much that his mouth hangs open and froths. When he resists a jointed snaffle, he often opens his mouth, pushing his jaw to one side to defeat the nutcracker action. Unfortunately, some riders mistake the first action for the second, think that any open mouth means resistance, and strap their horses' mouths shut with severe nosebands. These, of course, prevent the horse from truly accepting the bit. The real function of a noseband is to anchor a standing martingale, a strap running to the girth to prevent the horse raising his head too high.

Other gadgets and devices that force the horse's nose in are generally counter-productive, for they usually produce repressed tension rather than acceptance. There is no substitute for patient retraining, gentle hands, and thoughtful understanding.

Working together

Whatever you want to do with your horse, whether it be win the Olympics, cross a continent or simply have fun, you will find these same principles apply. Only when he moves forward freely does he develop power; only when he has power can he be rebalanced; only when his balance is good can he be light and responsive.

You have also seen that he cannot or will not respond when he is tense or miserable. He is not an automaton, but a living, feeling animal, whose emotions are quite as powerful as your own, though his logic is not. His language is complex and powerful, too, and he will tell you how he feels if you learn to listen and watch. Learning how to keep him in good health and spirits, to make sure his tack fits well, his food and surroundings suit him, and his feet do not hurt are also essential parts of horsemanship.

You will also, inevitably, have to think about how to teach a horse what you want. He is not born with mysterious knowledge about how you want him to behave. What he knows instinctively is about companionship and escape from wolves. He has no concept of obedience or naughtiness, or that you think your word is law. He *reacts*. When you ask him to move and it is pleasurable for him, he repeats the action happily. When it is not pleasurable, he tries another solution. If nothing seems to work, he tries to escape. Watch badly ridden horses and you will see that most of their energy is directed towards escaping or at least ignoring their riders.

This means that reward (a moment's peaceful rest is a reward, too) and praise are the most effective means of training. When you ask something of a horse, do it in a way that causes him no tension, pain or fear. When he starts to respond, praise and encourage him; rest for a

moment; and repeat the lesson. Repeat it again every few days for a couple of weeks; after that he will not forget.

If he does not respond, ask yourself why not. Is he physically fit enough? Supple enough? Comfortable? Are you using your aids calmly and accurately, in a way that he can understand? Or is he ignoring you? If he is, simply persist, gently, until he realizes he will have no peace until he listens.

Punishment and pain play no part in teaching except, occasionally, when a young horse bites. If biting you hurts him, he will not repeat it; but he connects the pain with what he is doing at the moment, not what he was doing two seconds before. If you are not quick enough, you will only annoy and puzzle him. Far too many horses are hurt by bossy, foul-tempered and ignorant riders. If you hit a horse for refusing a jump, you may terrorize him into escaping over that jump, but he will learn to hate jumping and everything associated with it, including you on his back.

In teaching, take your time. A horse needs time to think, to let his learning sink in. Sometimes he needs more time to develop muscle, suppleness and agility. Be patient. Set your sights high, but be content with any move in the right direction. Your patience will pay off, for your horse will increasingly enjoy working with you and take an interest in your odd ideas. This is true partnership, whatever style it may take. 'Such are the horses on which gods and heroes ride', Xenophon said.

Good horsemen throughout the ages have never ceased to wonder at, and be grateful for, the privilege of working so closely with an alien creature. Their attitude made them humble, thoughtful and delighted. If that is yours, you too will ride well.

Glossary

Throughout this book an effort has been made to avoid technical terms, for they are often glibly or inaccurately used. Among the commoner ones are the following:

Cadence. Increased spring or lilt given when the stride is shortened and the moment of suspension (*q.v.*) is increased, so the horse seems to hang in the air. Cadence without rhythm is unthinkable, though rhythm without cadence is often seen.

Central seat. Term used in this book for the general, balanced seat with stirrups just short enough to allow the rider to rise from the saddle. In the United States of America called the 'full' seat.

Centre of gravity. Balance point of any body or object. The horse's centre of gravity moves forward or back as his body changes shape. Here this has been called 'his see-saw going down in front' or 'shifting his balance backward', which you can feel.

Collection. In collection the horse shifts his balance backward; carries more weight on his hind legs; shortens his back; raises his loins; drops his rump; brings his hind legs further forward and closer together, with the joints more bent; shortens and arches his neck by flexing at the poll. Collected paces are marked by a complete lack of tension or resistance; springy, elastic co-ordination; cadenced strides in proud self-carriage (*q.v.*); contained impulsion (*q.v.*).

Contact. Connection between the rider's hands with the horse's mouth via the reins. Perfect contact is only possible when the horse carries himself in balance without support from the reins. There should be no weight on the reins, yet the horse should lengthen his stride when the rider moves his hands forward. If he does not, he is behind the bit (see page 106).

Deep seat. Sitting right down on the horse by spreading your legs wide and relaxing them. Sometimes 'sit deep' is used to mean 'brace your back' (see page 59).

Engaging the hocks. Lowering the rump and bringing the hocks further under the body so that they are more bent in all phases of the stride.

European riding. Term used in this book for the style of riding based on the classical use of aids, as opposed to Western-style riding. In the United States generally called 'English' riding.

Extended paces. Longer strides with increased engagement of the hocks. Merely lengthening the stride is not extending it.

Impulsion. Forward-going power produced by energetic hindquarters; willingness to release stored energy. Thus a horse can have impulsion even at a standstill.

Lateral movements. Movements in which the horse's hind feet do not follow his front ones, e.g. shoulder-in.

Moment of suspension. Moment when all the horse's feet are off the ground. Longer in cadenced paces.

Near side. Horse's left.

Off side. Horse's right.

On the bit. Willing to respond to the slightest change in the rider's hand, through being well balanced and in self-carriage (*q.v.*). It does not mean that the horse is pressing on the bit: he is 'on' the bit as you are on the telephone or on the alert, not as on a weighing machine.

Overbent. With the nose brought in behind the vertical through bending half-way down the neck rather than at the poll. Flexion at the poll helps shorten the horse's back; flexion in the neck does not. Seen when the horse is behind the bit (see page 106) or when the curb is over-used.

Outline. Shape of the horse's body along his top-line, from his nose to his tail. Attention to outline tends to lead to too much concentration on head position rather than on how the horse is using his body: look instead at his loins, his rump and where his back feet land. Horses of different natural shape carry their heads differently even in perfect collection.

Power. The horse's power can only be realized to the full when proper balance is achieved, as explained in *The Fourth Principle* (pages 96-146).

Rhythm. Regularity of rhythm is a prerequisite of higher training; the same rhythm is maintained through all tempos.

Self-carriage. Seen when the horse holds himself in good balance without support from the reins.

Tempo. Distance covered in a given time. In extension the tempo increases but the rhythm should not.

Works quoted

François Baucher, *Méthode d'Equitation*, 1842; Federico Caprilli, *Per l'Equitazione di Campagna*, 1901; Alexis l'Hotte, *Questions Equestres*, 1906; Duke of Newcastle, *General System of Horsemanship*, 1743; Nuno d'Oliveira, *Reflections on Equestrian Art*, 1964; Antoine Pluvinel, *Le Manège du Roi*, 1625; Xenophon, *On Horsemanship*, 4th century BC, republished 1987.

Index

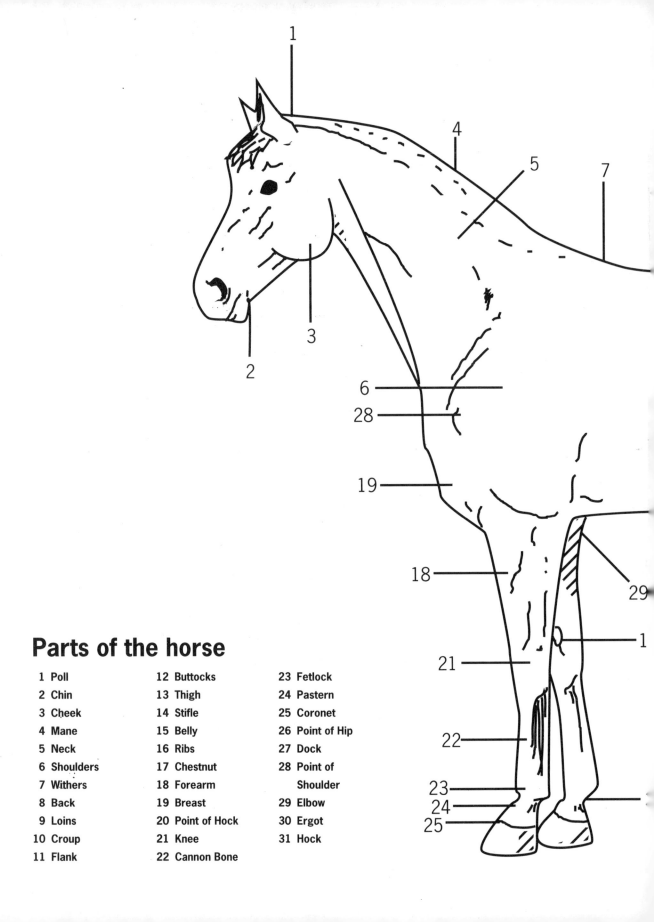

Parts of the horse

1 Poll	12 Buttocks	23 Fetlock
2 Chin	13 Thigh	24 Pastern
3 Cheek	14 Stifle	25 Coronet
4 Mane	15 Belly	26 Point of Hip
5 Neck	16 Ribs	27 Dock
6 Shoulders	17 Chestnut	28 Point of
7 Withers	18 Forearm	Shoulder
8 Back	19 Breast	29 Elbow
9 Loins	20 Point of Hock	30 Ergot
10 Croup	21 Knee	31 Hock
11 Flank	22 Cannon Bone	